QUIET AS KEPT

SHAWNTI REFUGE

DEDICATION

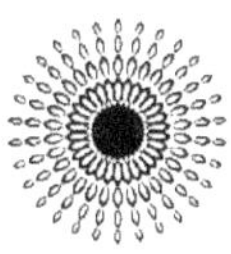

I give all the glory and honor to God, who I reconnected with during my healing process and who never left my side, even when I chose to believe that He did. He kept me through it all and is still fighting my battles and vindicating me for all the pain, embarrassment, lies, and betrayal that I have endured!

It is with great pleasure that I dedicate this book to my wife, Angela, who was with me during the worst part of my life. She stuck by me through the trauma and healing process. She was strong for me when I wasn't. I love you, Pooh.

ACKNOWLEDGEMENTS

God. Shawnti. Mom. Dad. Rosie. Papaw. My children. Ieshia. Briana. Kamilah Thomas, LSCW. Angela Refuge. Tawanna. D-tra. Pastor Kim Jones. Limitless Church. RTK Inner Circle. Dr. Candace Walters. Tammy Johnson. Robbi. Tiffany Green.

VIII

TABLE OF CONTENTS

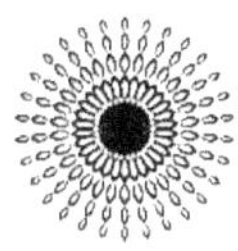

INTRODUCTION

My life experiences have inspired me to write this book because other people might be experiencing or have experienced similar things, and I hope that I can help someone push through their pain by sharing mine.

My name is Shawnti Refuge. This book contains information that may trigger some individuals. It definitely will make somebody mad, but I don't care. I've held it in for so long; now is my time to let it out. You are about to read real-life accounts of MY LIFE, as told by ME. Some names have been omitted to maintain the privacy of those involved, although they don't deserve it. I am a lady, so I will continue to carry myself as such. Hit dogs will always holler. Just know that these situations really happened. Nothing you are about to read is exaggerated. Everything that you are about to read will make you feel something, whether it's laughter, sadness, or anger. This shit is real.

Chapter
ONE

EARLY LIFE

I'm from Beaumont, Texas, a small town about 81 miles outside Houston. I was born and raised there. My dad named me after his Army buddy. His name was Shawnti, and it means peace. I didn't learn this until I was an adult. Looking back, my childhood wasn't the greatest. From what I can remember, I spent most of my time with my grandmother, whom I adored. My mom worked, and when she wasn't working, she went out on weekends with friends. I remember waiting for her to come through the door after a night out. She was the most beautiful woman in the world to me, and I wanted to be just like her.

My mother and I didn't have a great relationship as I became older. She was a young mother. She had me when she was 20. My dad was young, too. They were high school sweethearts. I've never seen my mom and dad together as a couple. They divorced when I was two years old. From what I was told, we used to live in California. I don't remember that, but I have seen pictures from when we lived out there. My dad was in the Army, so he traveled a lot. I've heard that my mom left my dad while we were in California because she wanted to move back home to Beaumont to be closer to my grandmother. She was the youngest, so she was the baby and wanted to return home where it was familiar. Let my dad tell it: my mom left because she no longer loved him. Boy, was he wrong.

At the time, I thought my mom was a great mother sometimes. I equated her greatness with always having what I needed physically, like clothes, shelter, and food. She was physically abusive and in a physically abusive relationship for a while after she married for the second time. I remember her being with her second husband; he was physically abusive towards her, and I used to get my ass kicked all the time. Looking back, she was taking her frustrations out on me because she couldn't defend herself against her abusive husband. She eventually left him and ended up with another man. Here enters my little sister, who is six years younger than me. I thank God she didn't have a kid with that second husband. He recently died. May he rot in Hell.

I used to think that my little sister was my baby. I got to name her and everything, but things quickly changed when I started being ignored by my mom. Now that I'm an adult, I was jealous of my little sister. She got all of the attention, and I got none. To me, she got everything she wanted. Her dad was in her life. I wasn't getting it either. Yes, I know this is a normal feeling, but mine was taken to the extreme, leading to us not getting along for most of our childhood.

At the time, my dad wasn't physically present in my life because he was traveling due to his demanding duties in the Army that required him to be away from me, so I assumed. Later, I found out he traveled due to the woman he was with whom he later married, then divorced some years later. (He told me this when I was an adult.)

I would refer to him as my telephone dad because he used to call me all the time, and he used to provide for me financially, but I never really saw him in person. I used to see him once a year. It would either be me going to see him or he would come to see me, depending on the circumstances. He wasn't nurturing like a father, although I didn't know what that was then. I just knew he wasn't it.

It was my greatest joy to spend time with my grandmother, who did not want to be called grandma, mom, or anything like that. Rosie is what she wanted to be called, so that is what I called her. She raised me and has always been kind to me, even as a child when I didn't deserve it. She always treated me with the kindness you were supposed to give a kid. We had a great relationship. I miss her so much. She passed away when I was 20.

If I could describe myself, I would say I'm smart, independent, stubborn, determined, and an overachiever who's always out to prove someone wrong about me. I can be mean sometimes. I can also come off as uncaring. I am also, at times, nonchalant, and I still have that tendency. I blame the Aquarius in me. It's either that or a defense mechanism. As I got older, I always said I would never be like my mom. Now that I've said that, I realize how much I can be like her, and I wouldn't say I like it. When I say that, I don't mean she's a bad person because she's not. She can be too giving and definitely to the wrong people. She's also an avoider, especially of essential things. I've been getting better and not adopting the same traits she has. I think, in some ways, I am like my grandmother too: kind, giving, selfless.

Growing up, there was no affection. I didn't know what that was. We didn't say, "I love you," or hug each other. My mother didn't do hugs, but my grandmother did. I thought this was normal at the time.

We didn't sit at the dinner table and discuss our day like the families did on TV. I wanted to live like that. Hell, I wasn't asked about anything, not even my grades. Until a few years ago, I still didn't talk about my feelings to anybody. I felt weird at the thought of even sharing my feelings with anyone. I kept it to myself because that's what I knew. That's what I thought I was supposed to do: keep it all in and push through.

Once, I remember we were at my grandmother's house, but my grandmother wasn't there. My stepdad, who used to abuse my mom, and I were the only ones there. My mom had not yet arrived. Sometime during the day, I told my stepdad I wanted to call my dad, and he allowed me to do so. He told my mom when she got back, "She wanted to talk to her daddy, so we called him." She got so furious that she kicked me out the door with her feet, and one of the neighbors, Mr. Green, saw her. She never did that again after he told her that if she did it again, he would contact child protective services & tell my grandmother. I was no more than four years old. YES, I remember that clear as day.

When I was in the third grade, she got mad at me for something the day before the first day of third grade. I did or said something to get in trouble, but I don't remember what it was, but she was mad. She wore a belt with indentions in it. She took it off and motioned as if she would whip me, and I started running as any kid would when they saw pain coming. She made a motion like a whip cracking, and the belt caught me on the side of my face as I ran away. I cried, of course. That shit hurt. I kept feeling this stinging sensation, so I hopped up on the sink in the bathroom to look in the mirror to see why my face was stinging. Instead of circle loops on the belt, there were stars. A line of swollen stars and broken skin was on the left side of my face near my eye.

As a result, I went to school with a line of stars on my left cheek on the first day of third grade. I was so embarrassed, especially since my second-grade teacher came in to check on his previous-grade students. I turned my head when he entered the classroom so he wouldn't see it. I was hoping that he didn't say anything to me. He didn't.

There was no verbal apology from my mom when she did me wrong, but she did offer me food as an apology. Now that I think about it, giving me food was her way of apologizing whenever she wronged me as a kid. That's probably why I was a chubby kid. That time she hit me across the face, her boyfriend at the time (my middle sister's dad) said, "Don't you think you hit her too hard?" She told him she would hit me harder than that next time. After that, she thought about it and came and gave me a popsicle. That was her way of saying she was wrong, I guess.

My mom wasn't all bad. During my childhood, I did have happy moments, like when I was in dance. Yes, I was in tap, jazz, ballet, and gymnastics. I loved it all. For the longest time, I wished I never quit dancing. Shit, I still wish I never left. I probably would be a dance teacher or own a dance studio somewhere.

I made sure I was the best dancer in class. I used to get all the solos and would be in the front for the group dances, and some of the other girls were mad. I remember when the teacher heard two of the girls teasing me and calling me fat. She was so upset she held a conference with the parents and my mom. I had no idea they didn't like me. I didn't even hear them talking about me. I wasn't bothered either when I did find out. I knew I was a better dancer than them, and they were jealous. To this day, I wish I would have kept dancing. I'm sure my life would have turned out much differently, but everything happens for a reason.

I knew I was favored in dance class. I loved it. My teachers were always friendly to me and encouraging. That's something I didn't get at home. So why in the hell did I stop going to dance class? MIDDLE SCHOOL is why. My dumb ass thought I was too old to be taking a dance class. I just quit going. No one in my family encouraged me or made me continue dancing. More on that later…

The resentment I felt towards my mother impacted how I was a mother to my children, as I found myself doing some of the same things my mom did to me regarding not showing much affection toward them. Let's be clear. I didn't abuse them, but I did discipline them. We'll get into that later too.

There was a time when my mom and I didn't speak. I didn't call her for two years when I moved to Houston. I had so much anger built up towards her, and I blamed her for so many things that went wrong in my life that I just needed my space from her.

That's something I've always said. My plan was to get out of Beaumont and away from my mom when I turned 18. That's exactly what I did. I never got along with her during my childhood. So, in other words, when I moved to Houston, I was like, I'm grown, and I don't have to talk to you anymore.

Over the next two years, I did not communicate with her. One day, I decided, okay, let me talk to my mom. Anyway, my mother and I have started a relationship again, and we talk, though we have never been the best of friends. Now that I am a full-grown woman, I know we will never be because we are not on the same page, and that's unfortunate.

We have this weird relationship right now, and I don't know what to call it. Because she still triggers me, so I take her in doses. She doesn't provide motherly support. I can't talk to her about my thoughts, feelings, or issues because everyone in Beaumont would know about it. How do I know? Because any time my sisters tell her something in confidence, she tells me about it. I learned a long time ago not to tell her my business.

Whenever I went to my aunt and uncles for the summer as a kid, they would take me and my cousin on trips, and we would go to AstroWorld or the beach. Those are my favorite childhood memories. Those were the times that I felt loved, cared for, important, and free like a kid should. I miss those days, sometimes. Those people from back then aren't the same today.

I had a friend in middle school who spent the night at my house. You know, like girls would in middle school. My mind goes back to a time when we were sharing secrets. I confessed to her that I thought I had sex with this guy and thought I was pregnant. Yes, I thought, because I didn't know what sex was then. She told her mom, and her mom called my mom and told her what I said. I remember walking into the house one day to my mama kicking my ass. All I know is that she hung up the phone and started kicking my ass. She never told me why she was doing it. I had no clue what I'd done or what I was being punished for.

I discovered the next day at school because my mom kicked my ass. This friend had told someone my secret, who then came and told me. I knew it was true because only my friend knew what I said. She couldn't even face me. We never spoke again. I never said anything to her and completely shut her out after that. There was no point in confronting her. She knew what she did. Even if there were good intentions behind it, she didn't realize that her mom and my mom were different. I couldn't talk to my mom about anything. Apparently, she could. This turned me into the type of person who can completely be done with you once you have done me wrong. I can say hi and be friends with you, but I will erase you when you do something to me. And that's what I did.

Let me tell you how backward I used to be. Initially, I gave everyone the benefit of the doubt; I trusted them 100% right off the bat. My ignorance back then would lead to me taking some of my trust away as they did things instead of making them earn it. I didn't know any better because I wasn't taught any better. I was young, naive, uneducated, and dumb when it came to social relationships and boundaries.

During middle school, I wanted to be liked so much that I did whatever I could, almost to the point of selling my soul, not being myself, but doing what people wanted me to do and giving them what they wanted. I thought that's what you were supposed to do because I wasn't taught any different. I wasn't taught about self-respect, self-love, self-worth, or self-esteem. I learned all this the hard way.

I began wetting the bed at six years old. I wasn't doing it on purpose. It just happened while I was sleeping. It wasn't every night, but damn near. It was not only frustrating for me but for my mom, too. She's the one who had to wash the sheets. She got so frustrated with me wetting the bed that she used to whip me for it. She thought I was being lazy and not wanting to get up and go to the restroom at night.

It took her YEARS to understand that I wasn't doing it on purpose, finally. After many years of ass whippings and new mattresses, she tried to get me help but couldn't afford it. I remember a white lady coming to our apartment with a video presentation about a blanket you put on the bed, and if I started wetting the bed, an alarm would go off and wake me up. I don't know how safe that was, but I didn't get one. Thank you, Jesus.

I remember in middle school, all I wanted was a boyfriend, or so I thought. I used to wonder why none of the boys would talk to me. I later found out by a male classmate why. He said, "Shawnti, all the boys be trying to talk to you. They asked your cousin to hook them up, but he told them, 'You don't want to talk to her. She pees in the bed.'" I could tell he wasn't telling me to be funny. He was telling me because he knew it was wrong. My heart sank. How could my cousin rat me out like that? I never told anyone he peed in the bed, too. I kept his secret. I never talked to him again after that; my cousin, that is.

My classmates didn't like me, regardless of how I behaved. I just found myself getting used to every sense of the word. I was getting abused sexually, financially, morally, talked about, bullied; you name it, it happened. Kids can be fucking cruel. I didn't know how to defend myself either. I was too busy trying to find out why no one liked me, or so I thought. Enter self-loathing.

I excelled in my classes, but you wouldn't know it because of how I portrayed myself. Back then, the smart kids were teased for being smart, so I acted dumb. I was the troublemaker, the class clown. In essence, I dimmed my light so that I would not blind others. I did not want to stand out; I tried to blend in and be like everyone else, but that never worked out for me.

During my early years as a student, I used to get frustrated when I didn't get an A or a B on a test. I used to feel that I had to surpass everybody in the class. It was my goal to be the most intelligent person in the class. Whenever I didn't get an A when I thought I should, I literally cried. My heart was broken.

In elementary school, I remember coming home crying when I got a B in a class and my mother telling me, "Shut up, at least you passed." Was my mother telling me to be mediocre? I said yes, but I wasn't trying to hear that. I was never satisfied with good enough. I'm still not.

As a result of doing things to make other people like me, I felt like I wasn't wanted as I was, whoever I was. I never got invited to sleepovers or birthday parties like the other kids, so I started getting frustrated and wondering what was wrong with me. After returning to school on some Mondays, I heard about different events others had attended or how classmates spent time together. I wondered why the fuck I wasn't invited to anything. What was wrong with me that no one liked me or wanted to be around me? That just made me angry on the inside—Que in low self-esteem.

Oh, and the one time I got invited to a party, I got an anonymous phone call a few hours before telling me not to come because I would get jumped. In the sixth grade, at the time, I knew that someone called my house, but I had no idea who it was. The party was happening on a Friday night. I was excited to be invited to my first party. After that phone call, I decided not to go because I didn't want to get jumped. I was scared. I never fought before. I didn't have anyone who would help me if I did get jumped. I just knew it was girls, and they went to school with me.

It confused me. What makes me wonder is why somebody would want to jump me. I didn't do anything wrong to anyone. If I did, I wasn't aware. I was mad because I already had my outfit picked out, and I was excited to go somewhere. Because it was embarrassing, I never told my mom why I was no longer attending the party. I just told her I changed my mind and didn't want to go.

My desire to belong led me to have sex for the first time at 12 when I had no idea what sex was. At the time, I had no idea how it worked. I was never educated on what sex was nor the potential consequences of it. I used to ask my mom, "What is sex?" As a kid, I had no clue. "Don't do it" was all I was told. In my mind, "Hmmm, let me see what it is that she doesn't want me to do."

Probably one of the main reasons I didn't realize that I was having sex for the first time was the fact that I didn't feel anything at the time. It was more like the person I was having sex with was having sex with me. We were in a public park restroom. I know, it's disgusting. The feeling was almost like I was just there physically, but apart from that, it didn't seem like anything special. Thinking back, I now know he just had a little dick. He was older than me (in 8th grade) and knew I was a virgin. Maybe he thought I wouldn't be able to tell the difference. I couldn't at the time, but I was wondering why the other girls would say it hurt and you bleed, and I didn't do either.

I was told by the boy who I had sex with that this is the best way to show someone that you love them. In other words, if you love me, prove it by having sex with me. My young, naive ass believed him. I mean, why not? I didn't have a man in my life to tell me any different. I thought this was how it was supposed to be. At the time, if I could do anything differently, I would have gone straight home after school and not lied and told my mom I had choir practice. It definitely wasn't worth it. Then, after he got it, he called me a hoe. I didn't even know what a hoe was then, but it wasn't a good thing.

Between sixth and eighth grade, I'd been called many things: hoe, pissy, dirty, nasty, and probably more that hadn't gotten back to me. Most girls didn't like me. I had no friends from school. I let people use and bully me. I didn't know any better, and no one knew what was happening in my family. I pretended as best I could that everything was fine. I guess I didn't do it well because I developed anger issues. I remember when my grandfather told my mom to take me to a psychiatrist, and she would get mad. I wish she would have listened.

GROWING UP

When I was 14 and in 8th grade, I got pregnant, and that was my worst memory as a child. At the time, I was in eighth grade and the child's father was a senior in high school. He used to always come to the apartment complex I lived in to see me. My friend at the time hooked us up.

I was in a relationship with a classmate that she didn't like, so she used this guy that she knew to distract me to get away from my current boyfriend. I didn't learn this until later. Hell, my boyfriend at the time wasn't a boyfriend. I was only with him to say I had a boyfriend. People used to tell me that he was telling people that the only reason he was with me is because he heard fat girls got good pussy.

Of course, they do, especially when the guy has yet again a little dick. We had sex one time. He got up and said, "It's over." I said, "I know." I never caught feelings for the dudes I was having sex with. I treated them all as something to do until…

When it came to him being older than me, I thought it made me seem like I was all that. I felt like I was the shit because I had an older "man". I just knew he was going to take care of me. I can't help but laugh while writing this. Keep in mind that back then, I was looking at it from the perspective of an 8th grader. As an adult, looking back, boy, was I stupid. To this day, I always tell my mom that she should have hit me upside the head with a frying pan, and she shouldn't have let me talk to this old dummy.

I remember one day; I skipped school to be with him. We rode the city bus to his house. Yeah, this "man" didn't have a car. That was my first time ever riding the city bus. I never needed to before then. When we got to his house, he told me to wait in the front and went around to the back. I didn't know his mama was home. While waiting in the front, I could feel someone peering out the window behind me. I was too scared to look. His mama caught us, and she said to me, "I don't know why you are fucking with him because he ain't shit." I didn't believe her. She didn't know how young I was. In my mind. I was like, "Why would somebody say that about their own kid?" I should have listened because he wasn't shit then, and he ain't shit now.

We were together for, I'd say, three months. I was happy as fuck. He really seemed like he was into me. I used to sneak him into the house and skip school to be with him. I did all kinds of stupid shit for him in that little amount of time, including lying and stealing. I remember that summer, I had to go and visit my dad in Maryland, and I cried because I did not want to go. I knew that if I went, I would lose him. Thank God I went because he wasn't nothing to lose. As a matter of fact, when I was in Maryland, one of my friends who I had watching him called me. She told me that he had another girlfriend and that he bought her a cookie cake and a balloon bouquet for her birthday. You might as well have put a dagger in my heart because he never gave me anything but a baby and a STD.

When I found out, I was around 5 or 6 months pregnant. It was 1991. My grandmother took me to my pediatrician because, eventually, someone noticed that I wasn't having my period. So, when we found out, I told the father, and his response was that it wasn't his. I felt worthless. I was already scared and crying because, oh my God. I was thinking, I am only in the eighth grade; what am I going to do with a baby? I thought to myself, "What am I doing pregnant? What are people going to think of me? How am I going to take care of a baby? I don't want this damn baby!" For most of my pregnancy, I cried. That's probably why my baby was a crybaby.

My grandmother told my mom, but I was more scared of what my grandmother thought than anything. And she didn't treat me any differently. She said, "I still love you; people make mistakes," and she reassured me it would be okay. I probably would have lost my mind if it weren't for her. All I remember was crying on the table when the doctor examined me, and even when he told me I was pregnant, I was denying it. I was denying it so much that he did an internal examination and said you're about five or six months pregnant. I fuckin died. I cried out of the doctor's office, to the car, and to the house, where I ran in my grandmother's room, jumped in her bed, and cried. I could not stop crying. I was so upset, ashamed, and scared. I was crying. I just knew that my mama was going to whip my ass literally.

I could not think of a name for this new baby: a girl. So, I let her dad name her. He came around a little bit after the birth to sign the birth certificate and accept that he was the father. Other than that, my baby's father was never there. He didn't help with anything, and he barely came around. His mom finally came around when I was in the 10th or 11th grade. She would get the baby every now and again. But for the most part, it was just me, my mom, and my grandmother.

I never wanted a baby. I always said I didn't want to have kids because I don't like kids. When my family found out I was pregnant, my aunt and uncle, who used to take me to AstroWorld when I was younger, said they wanted to adopt my baby, and I agreed. Initially, I was supposed to get an abortion, but I chickened out. I was like, "Nah, don't get one." My dad sent me the money to get one, but I changed my mind about it. I got my hair and a new outfit with the money he sent me to get an abortion.

We were making arrangements for my aunt and uncle to get the baby, and once I had her, I changed my mind about that, too. I was like, "No, I'm keeping my baby," because I could only picture it coming out at Thanksgiving 20 or 30 years later. I was thinking, what if somebody exposes the secret and says that ain't your cousin, daughter, or you know your mom or something? Because that's how my family is. That's how the elders who are supposed to set the examples are anyway.

At the time when I had the baby, my mom just got laid off from her job, and she became my babysitter. She had been laid off from her job for over 20 years, and that's all she knew. I could tell she was upset about it, but she didn't talk about it, and I didn't know what that meant for us. Again, I was young, and I didn't understand. I didn't return to school for about two months because I was doing home school. Back then, they gave you a choice of when you came back to school or if you wanted to be homeschooled. Now that I look back on it, that was God working because he knew that I was gonna need someone to care for my baby when I went back to school, and there was no one. I didn't want to put that on my grandmother, so my mom got laid off just at the right time, right before I went into labor, and she ended up being my babysitter for a year.

The baby and I never wanted for anything. My mom helped me get the resources that the baby and I needed, such as WIC and TANF. So, I thought life was fine. Keep in mind back then, it was 1991, so things were a lot cheaper and more easily accessible.

Before I had the baby, my classmates didn't see me until I was in the 9th grade. My stomach was big. I would have people come up to me saying, "Shawnti, you pregnant? You're pregnant?"

I wouldn't even answer them. I would just keep walking. You could definitely see I was pregnant. But after I went away and had my baby and came back, people didn't fuck with me. They even had a class back then for girls who were either pregnant or who had babies. I can remember the school nurse walking me to my new class and telling me, "Baby, don't be ashamed. You're not the only one who is pregnant." As we were walking to the building where my new class was, all I could think about was what I was gonna walk into. Who was I going to see? I was surprised to see all the girls in there who either already had their babies or were pregnant. I didn't feel alone anymore. I was surprised to see a couple of girls in there who I never knew were pregnant. They had already had their babies, and they were younger than me. I was fourteen when I had my baby. These girls were 12 and 13. There were a few other girls in there who were pregnant or already had a kid and were pregnant again, and we were all in the 9th grade.

The same friend who hooked me up with this man also influenced me to act out when I was that age. I was weak-minded as fuck, if you couldn't tell already. I wish someone would have told me not to hang around her or at least to have a mind of my own. I got in 80% of my troubles by hanging around her. But she was intriguing and fun. Yes, I know I had a mind of my own and could make my own choices. She was everything I was missing in my life, or so I thought. She made her life look so exciting, and I wanted that life. It was all fun and games until she referenced me as her shadow in one of our classes. She distinctly said, "Hey, y'all look at my shadow." And I can't even hate on that because she was right; I was doing everything she was doing. The difference was either she was lying about what she was doing and had me believing it, or she was doing it and wasn't getting caught. My dumb ass was always getting caught.

When I was in the 10th, 11th, and 12th grades of high school, I was done trying to be liked and invited. I was like, fuck all y'all. I walked around with a chip on my shoulder. My grades were falling. I no longer cared about being the best. I just wanted to get by. My main goal in life at that time was to graduate from school. That's all I cared about. In my mind, I said when I graduate, I'll be grown, and I'm moving out of Beaumont.

In terms of friendships, I finally gained a real best friend. To this day, we remain friends. Back then, both of us were teen moms. In high school, we met in one of those pregnancy classes. However, she was older than me. She rolled her eyes at me when we first met. We didn't like each other. However, we were confined to that class. We bonded through talking about our children. As a result, we became best friends after getting to know each other and talking to each other. It turned out that she lived around the corner from me. Whenever she was at my house, she would always have her baby with her. Therefore, they spent more time at our house than at hers. We relied on each other since she didn't talk to people either. We used to get in trouble together. We actually got arrested together. That's my ride-or-die.

Yes, I got arrested when I was 16 for shoplifting out of this store called Montgomery-Ward. My best friend and I used to hit up all the stores in the mall and come out with all kinds of stuff. We didn't have to shoplift, but we did it out of boredom. Well, let me speak for myself: I did it out of boredom. I'm the type of person who loves a challenge. It was challenging to be able to go into a store, get what I wanted, and get out with it. Whatever I took from the stores, I would sell them. I was even taking orders from classmates who wanted things, and I would go get it and sell it to them for half price. I remember I used to hit up this department store and the mall, take all their Dooney bags, and sell them at the Washateria. It was fun for me until the one day we got caught.

I remember it like it was yesterday. We were in Montgomery Ward, and we loaded up and were getting ready to go. We almost made it to the car when I heard a man say, "Ladies, I need you to come back inside." We all were looking around like who is he talking to. That was my way of being in denial about getting caught because he couldn't have seen me. Apparently, a store clerk saw me and reported us. They initially reported that I stole a bra and panty set, which I did, but when they searched my bag,

I had a whole wardrobe that they didn't even know I had. So, they took their report, a police car came and got us, and we were on our way to jail.

We were in a holding cell for about 12 hours, and then we went to court that morning. Because I was sixteen, I was in the juvenile court. My best friend was older than me; she was seventeen, almost 18, so they sent her to adult court. I was so upset when they separated us because I didn't know what was going to happen. We did everything together; this was the first time that we were being separated by force. My middle sister's dad came to court to support me. My mom didn't want to come because she didn't want to be involved. She was scared that she was going to lose her job. I remember when they called my name to come up, I was nervous as hell. The judge read what I was charged with and asked me how I plead. I said I was guilty because I was. There was no need to lie about it. The judge proceeded to tell me that either I had to pay a $250 fine or spend 30 days in jail. I remember looking back at my sister's dad with my eyes, saying get me out of here. They led me to the back and put me in a holding cell. At that time, I never knew what happened to my friend, so I was really worried about her. About an hour or two later, a policeman called my name and opened the cell. He brought me up to where they were doing fingerprints and taking mug shots. I remember when he took my mug shot, I smiled. I didn't smile because I was happy; I smiled because I was used to smiling when somebody had a camera in my face. Shit, I was nervous, and I always smile when I'm nervous.

This police officer looked at me and said, "I don't ever want to see you in here again. If I do, you will pay for it." At the time when he was saying it, I didn't know what he was talking about.

He told me to come with him, and I did. He walked me to a door, opened it, and ushered me out. I was standing outside in the free world, confused about what happened. I hurried up, ran to a payphone, and called my mom to collect because I didn't have a quarter. and I told her, "I need you to come get me." She didn't even let me finish my sentence before she cut me off and said, "I don't have any money to get you out; you're gonna have to stay in there." I was trying to tell her no, I'm free. I need a ride home. She wouldn't even come get me. My sister's dad came and got me.

My role model at that time was Mrs. Briggs. I don't even know what role she played in the school, but she started a program for kids who had kids, and in it, she paid for daycare and transportation so that people like me could continue their education. She wanted us to finish school. She cared about us.

I loved Mrs. Briggs. Several years ago, I was saddened to learn that she passed away. Her love for us was evident in the way she treated us. She always paid for if we weren't doing well in school and needed to attend summer school. I think it wasn't from her pocket, and I don't think she had to pay for it. She likely had grants or some other kind of assistance. Nevertheless, you know, she took good care of us, and many of us were in that group.

I wrote a letter to my 14-year-old self and wanted to share it with you all.

Dear 14-Year-Old Shawnti,

Although you were ashamed and worried about what your grandmother would think of your pregnancy, she never treated you differently. In fact, your parents and grandparents loved you equally and supported you throughout. You couldn't comprehend the consequences of what you were doing. You aren't entirely to blame for not being properly educated on sex. You didn't know that sex did not equal love. In fact, you didn't learn what love really was until much later in life. The love you received as a child was different. You needed more, and loving yourself was the first step. You didn't know about self-love and self-esteem at that time. All you know was that everyone else was doing it, or so you thought. And you thought that's what you were supposed to do. You just wanted to be liked. You wanted to have friends. You wanted to be popular. You never understood why no one liked you. You were nice to people, but all they did was talk about you. Even though you made bad choices, you persevered and completed your education. I'm proud of you for overcoming the obstacles that were in your life at that time. You are smart, and you are beautiful. You don't need validation from anyone. You will learn to be a better person for your child.

I remember the first time I wanted to go to a college party. I asked my mom if I could go, and her response was, "The damage is done, so you could do whatever you want." Boy, did I do whatever I wanted? My friend and I used to go to college parties, so many people thought we were in college because we did not look our age. We used to walk up and down the street at all times of the night, back and forth from parties to people's apartments to party. We were having so much fun, and I felt free. Where was my baby? She was with my momma.

After a while of partying, I got bored. So, I decided it was time for me to have a boyfriend. I asked my friend to hook me up with somebody, but they had to have a car and money. She introduced me to this one classmate when we were in the 11th grade. She told me he played football and had a car, and that's all she knew about him. I approached him one day at school and as if he wanted to talk. He told me he did not have time for a girlfriend because he focused on school and football. I could respect that, so I walked away. Then, he came up to me about a week later with a changed mind and decided that he did want to talk to me. So, we began talking. When I say talking, that is another way of saying getting to know each other, and eventually, we started dating.

Through dating, I found out that he was no longer in football because of his grades. I also found out that he got kept back because of his grades, so when I became a senior, he was a junior. I didn't care, though he had a car. He used to take me out on dates, and I loved it. I later discovered that I was his first girlfriend. I was his first everything, including sexual experience. I will admit he was a nice person and nice to be around. He wasn't disrespectful. If anything, I was the aggressor in the relationship, meaning that I called the shots. If I told him to walk on water, he would have or would have found a way to. It was fun at first, but then it got boring. After almost two years of dating, I started getting bored. Back then, I didn't have the courage to let him know that I was bored, so I just cheated on him. We were together for nearly ten years, and during that whole time, I was cheating on him.

After going to a career day at school in 10th grade, I thought I wanted to be a nurse. I really didn't know what I wanted to be. I even thought I wanted to be a cosmetologist because I was good at doing hair. I could do some hair. I did French rolls, cornrows, braids, weaves, and more. Hey, it was the 90s, so all those styles were in. I used to do my own hair. I also did the kids' hair in my neighborhood, so I thought I wanted to do that, and my grandmother was a cosmetologist. I thought, OK, I want to be like my grandma and be a cosmetologist. I went to cosmetology school, and I quit. I think I had an hour or two left to go to get my license. I just quit because I didn't want to do it anymore. I just couldn't see myself doing hair for the rest of my life. I just woke up one morning and said, "Fuck this." I left all of my cosmetology equipment at the school. I'm sure that made someone's day.

I had no clue what I wanted to do. All I knew was that I wanted to sit behind a desk. I knew I didn't want to work at any fast-food place; I didn't want to do any hard labor. I just knew I wanted to be sitting when I did whatever it was I did.

Growing Up

THE REAL WORLD

It was 1995, and I finally made it to 12th grade. I was a senior in high school. I was so excited to be graduating. I did not want any party, I didn't want any yearbooks, I didn't want anything but my diploma so I could get the fuck out of Beaumont. I remember my dad came to my graduation, and we lived so close to where it was being held, we walked so we wouldn't have to deal with parking. In my mind, I just knew that when we were walking back home after graduation, I was going to come home to a car with a big red bow on it. Boy, was I ever wrong? There was no car, and there wasn't even a graduation gift from my mom. My dad wrote me a check as he usually would do. I was so disappointed because I expected a car. Instead of getting a car, I later found out that I was gonna have a baby sister. Boy, what a present. I was genuinely pissed. I didn't want a sister. I wanted a car!

After I graduated from high school in 1995, I took the advice of my dad. At the time, he told me to take a year off. I couldn't believe he told me to do that, but I sure did listen to him because he was my dad, and I knew he would not steer me wrong. That was the worst thing I could have done because it put me behind. I got lazy. I didn't work. I didn't do shit for a whole year. I wasted a year of my life and probably gained 100 pounds because I ate all day and watched TV.

After that year of eating my life away, I enrolled at Lamar University in Beaumont. There was this program called Office Technology Administration. That's what I signed up for, in essence, to learn how to type and use computers and stuff and be somebody's secretary. At the time, I didn't know that the purpose of the class was to make you somebody's secretary, but afterward, I realized that's what it was. It was something I did not want to do, but I did want to learn how to use office software and equipment. It taught me how to use a computer, a fax machine, and all that stuff. So, I needed to learn how to do all of that. So, I took those courses.

I didn't finish school at all because it was dumb to me. So, the next semester, I changed what I wanted to do and ended up taking classes to be a news broadcaster. I only did it because one of my friends was doing it. We would take all the same classes together. And even though my boyfriend didn't graduate from high school, I convinced the Dean to admit him into college, so he was in college, too.

I ended up quitting again, and I started working as a cashier at Wendy's. I liked it until they asked me to make hamburgers, so I quit. Because I did not think I would get a degree soon, I decided to work for the post office instead. They didn't require much. I took the post office test and passed. I was always good at taking tests. I have the type of mind that I don't need to study to take a test; I would just take a test and pass it. So, I started working for the post office. Then I had it set in my mind this is where I'm going to retire. I worked there for about two years. I worked at night; I was not a carrier; I worked in processing. So, we would process the incoming mail on a computer. It was more like data entry and paid a lot of money back then. It was one of the highest-paying jobs in Beaumont at the time.

I worked there for two years. They announced that they were shutting down and they were offering us to move to Tennessee or Houston. I was young back then, and I was thinking, "Well, I'm not moving out of state. I don't know anybody there." So, I chose to apply to move to Houston. Right after I applied to move to Houston, they announced that they were doing a hiring freeze. I would have to reapply. I knew I didn't want to be a carrier; that was out of the question. I wanted to work inside the facility like I was currently doing. I stayed at the post office for as long as I could, and I started looking for jobs in Houston.

At the time, I wanted to move to Houston because I wanted to get away from Beaumont and the people there. Houston was a bigger city; I could be myself, and the jobs paid more there. Little did I know that the cost of living was higher, too, which is why the pay was higher.

I did not feel like I could be myself where I was because I didn't see any other gay people. At the time, I didn't know if there were any other gay people in Beaumont.

Around this time, I was about 21 or 22. I always had an attraction to women. Always. I remember watching a DJ Jazzy Jeff and the Fresh Prince's music video, and there was a close-up shot of someone's butt. I was in awe; however, I didn't know it was a girl. When they panned out on her, and I saw it was a girl,

I was like, Oh, shit. So that was a long time ago. Even when I would look at girls in the locker room, they'd probably die now if they knew. I never made any advancements toward them because I was afraid. All I knew was, you know, girl, boy, man, woman, you know, I didn't see anybody just being out as gay or lesbian.

I didn't see two males, two females, you know, I didn't see that growing up. So, I just kept it to myself. So, when I got to Houston, baby, my eyeballs were wide open. It was like a whole new world, and I was ready for it.

Back in Beaumont, I did what my mama wanted me to do. That meant I had to get really good at pretending or hiding who I really was at the time. I used to use dudes for sport. I was never interested in any of them. I remember a time that I fucked one dude just because I didn't like his girlfriend. I wasn't a very nice person back then.

I was living with my mom, so I was ready to get the hell out of there anyway. At the time, I only had one kid, so it was easy for me to move. I moved in with my aunt, who lives in Houston. So that was easy because she was happy for me to come. She's always been my favorite aunt. She was stern, but she loved us, and she showed us she loved us. Even though she told me that I was gonna be the one to have five different kids or one behind the other and I wasn't gonna graduate from school. So far, I have proven her wrong, and I was determined to prove her even more wrong.

When I moved, it was me, my baby, and my boyfriend at the time. I think one of my biggest regrets was taking him with me. I should have left him in Beaumont, but I brought him for the wrong reasons. I was in Houston for about six months, and then I told him to come. A decision I would regret for the rest of my life.

I met him when we were teenagers, and even though he had a car he was broke. However, his mother, who had money, gave it to him. He was a virgin but was into football and focused on school at the time, or so I thought.

He was a nice guy. I was a bad girlfriend to him. I cheated on him for most of the time we were together. I cheated because I wasn't satisfied sexually. At this point, I wasn't thinking of starting to be with women. I just thought, well maybe I will get what I need with another man. Come to find out, NO man satisfied me sexually. But that's a story for later.

When I told him I was cheating, he thought I was joking, because I used to play practical jokes on him all the time. He just questioned why I was cheating. He was sad, of course, because I was his first everything. I told him because I wanted him to break up with me, but he would not break up with me. I ended up getting pregnant. This was a little shocking because before he moved to Houston, I never got pregnant & we were fucking like rabbits. Once he moved in with me in Houston, I got pregnant. My mama told me that we needed to get married, and my stupid ass listened. I remember us getting married at the courthouse and my dad was there. When it came to my turn for me to say I do, I couldn't say it. I had to be nudged in order to say I do and even when I said I do, I did not mean it. I literally felt like I was signing my life away I felt like I was giving myself the death penalty. I went ahead with the wedding because I did not want to disappoint my dad. I was going to get an abortion because I didn't want another child. At the time I told one of my coworkers that I was pregnant and didn't want it, so she made me an appointment at what she thought was an abortion clinic. I went to the place, and it turned out to be one of those places that scared you into not getting an abortion.

Needless to say, they did their fucking job. In the end, I kept the baby, even though I didn't want it. We were married for about six months. I was tired of pretending with him and I'd had enough. I couldn't take it anymore, because I was not happy.

Chapter 3

UPS AND DOWNS

My postpartum depression was really, really bad after I had my second child. In those days, nobody knew what postpartum depression was. I stayed at home for about three months after I had the baby. Not only was I taking care of my baby, but I was also taking care of my best friend at the time. This person was a friend I met in Houston. My patience had run out. It was tiring for me. In addition to being a wife, I was tired of being a mother. I just wanted to run away. In hindsight I definitely wasn't ready for the life that I created. Better yet I did not want this life that I created for myself.

Before my baby was born, we lived in a one-bedroom apartment which was privately owned. Those apartments were similar to condominiums. We were also having issues with our neighbor downstairs. As a result, we decided to move somewhere else. So, I said, "Okay, we can't live in a one-bedroom, we need two." Furthermore, I wanted my older daughter to live with us again. She wanted to stay with my aunt when we moved to Houston and that was a stupid mistake.

The fact that my aunt had seven children made my daughter want to stay with her. They were all around the same age. She wanted to stay with her cousins, so she chose that option. I shouldn't have let a child make an adult decision and I would pay for that later in life. When I found out I was pregnant, I was like, okay, we'll have to move.

My daughter didn't understand why I was having another baby, but she still lives with my aunt. We were going to get a two-bedroom apartment so I could get my daughter back, and they'd just share a bedroom when the baby got older. We ended up relocating to a two-bedroom apartment, which was cheaper in rent.

When I was working at this job, I met this girl there, who was really cool, really carefree. After seeing her at the bus stop, I took her home a few times and we became friends. So, our friendship grew, we became strictly friends, nothing more. We went to parties and had a lot of fun together. I felt like she was the person I wanted to be. Basically, being carefree and just doing whatever she wants, not that she was reckless or anything, but just living her life. So, you know, that's why I latched on to her. Do you notice the pattern?

When I moved to Houston I hadn't been going to church because I didn't know what church to go. So, my friend took me to her church with her. For the longest time when I first started going, I could not understand anything they were saying. It's not that they weren't speaking English, they were but I just couldn't understand them because it sounded like Charlie Brown teacher. You know the "womp, womp, womp" one, that's literally how it sounded. After a few weeks of attending church, I finally was able to understand what they were saying. Of course, I kept that experience to myself because I didn't want to sound silly.

As we were moving into the two-bedroom apartment, she was getting evicted from her apartment, and she asked me if she could stay with us. I asked him about it, and he said he would be fine with it. Everything I told him to do, he did. He just wanted me to be happy and I can say that I took advantage of that. She stayed in the second bedroom, which was intended for my daughter. Eventually, I became attracted to my coworker after she was there for a while. During that time, I confided in my boyfriend that I was attracted to her. I told him, "Yeah, I'm into women." He said, "Alright." I was surprised that was his response because normally when a woman tells their boyfriend that they're into someone of the opposite sex it's normally a fight. There was no fight. He was okay. I want to say that he was ok because he thought he would be included, which was why he continued to let her stay, if you know what I mean.

My attitude towards him changed over time, and I wanted to send him back home to Beaumont. My attitude changed towards him for many reasons. Remember when I said he used to take me out, well he stopped doing that. He wasn't romantic. He actually started getting on my nerves. He couldn't keep his mama out of our business. One thing I can't stand is a mama's boy and he was that. I think my last straw was when our lights were turned off. While I was paying bills, he was writing checks, so the math wasn't mathing. Although, I didn't know how to tell him, I was afraid to say, "Look, I want you to go back to your mom because you aren't the man, I need you to be." I was afraid to tell him I wanted to be with a woman and not him. Plus, he used to have his sorry ass friends stay with us in this apartment. I didn't want them there either. I felt like we were a rooming house because the people were growing and growing but nobody was paying bills but me.

Despite this, I felt they could stay for a couple of weeks since he allowed her to come, but I just got tired of it and said fuck it. The first time my friend and I took it to another level was just by kissing. That's it. New Year's Eve was the night I shared my first kiss with her. That was my first time ever kissing a woman. At that point, I was like ok, yep, this is what I like. That kiss was like no other kiss I have ever experienced in life. I was 23 years old, and the year was 2001. I want to say she was 19 years old.

As time went on, I started sleeping in her bedroom with her. I used to leave him in our room with the baby. He used to try to get me into bed with him. I would tell him to leave me the hell alone. I just did not want to be in the bed with him my mind was made-up. After that kiss I felt like this is what I have been missing and not necessarily from her but from a woman period.

We weren't doing anything at that time. I just didn't want to be near him. I did not want to be with him physically, sexually, emotionally, or mentally. I did not want to have anything to do with him. I just did not know how to say it without hurting his feelings so I showed him better than I could tell him which in hindsight was the worst possible thing that I could have done to a person. He absolutely did not deserve what he got.

I don't remember the date, but I remember it was February 2002. I'd finally had enough. I was so sick of pretending to be a loving doting wife and mother. I was very unhappy in my situation, but I didn't have the nuts to say so. So, me and the girl, were in her room having sex while he was in our room with the baby.

It was late at night. they were asleep. I heard his two friends coming up the stairs and coming in the front door. That's when I made the decision to get "busted". I was purposely being loud, so they wouldn't mistake what they were hearing. Because I knew they were going to go tell him, and sure enough, they went and told him the next day. So, he asked, "Are you and such & such fucking?" And I said, yeah. In my opinion, he was more upset that he wasn't included, than the fact that I was cheating.

He still didn't get it, that I didn't want to be with him. I was forced to tell him, and I should have told him anyway. But I was forced to tell him, "Hey, it's over. I don't want to be with you anymore." So, I ended up just saying just that and he moved out maybe a week later.

I can tell you one thing; I was re-fucking-lieved! I said to myself, "Oh my God, what took you so long to open your mouth and just tell the truth? Why did it take you having a baby and getting married to this fool for you to come out and be yourself?" I felt like I wasted so much time. I actually did waste time; mine and his. However, going through this journey taught me a lot in the end.

He was understandably upset, furious even. I had him looking like a fool in front of his friends and family and everyone who knew us. I am not bragging about this. To be honest everyone knew about what I was doing except for him. It was just a matter of time before he found out and I did choose to let him find out the wrong way. I knew one day that I would have to pay for what I did. At the time I did not care I just was relieved and happy that I finally came out and it was over between us, or so I thought.

When he left after the incident, he also left his child. He didn't try to make any contact with me to get his child he didn't send any finances and at the time I wasn't even mad. I knew that I had broken him down, so I wasn't going to pressure him. I let him be for the time being. I wasn't happy about what I did but I was happy that I did it. If I could go back and do it the right way I would.

Ups And Downs

LOVE AND HAPPINESS

I thought I was in love with this woman. I was in love. Shit, she was my first lesbian relationship, so you know my nose eyes and ears was wide open. You couldn't tell me anything about this woman. The sun arose and set on her. I thought she was the most beautiful woman in the world. She was the one who taught me affection. I wasn't getting hugs and kisses and rubs on my back or anything like that. she was the first one to give that to me. Before her all I knew was sex. I didn't know love and affection an emotion. She was kind to me (in the beginning), and thoughtful, and very romantic and I ate it all up.

So, you know, we were making plans to live our lives together. Correction, I was making plans for us to be together. I wanted us to start fresh. So, we ended up moving to a new apartment. By this point, she had given birth to a little girl. Our girls were six months apart and it was just the four of us. I'm just as happy as I could be, and then she drops a bomb on me a year later that she wanted to work it out with her baby's father. I couldn't be mad at her for wanting to try to make it work so that her child could grow up with a father in the house. We all want that for our families. Hell, I thought I wanted it for my family.

I don't think it really hurt me that much because I knew she would be back. They always come back or at least; they always want to come back. I had that kind of mentality back then. We ended up getting separate apartments. She lived in her own apartment across the freeway, and I lived in my own apartment on the other side of the freeway. We were close, but not that close, you know? We still had keys to each other's apartments. Even though we weren't technically together, I still was adamant and showing her that I was the one she needed. I used my entire income tax check to decorate her apartment. I used to go to her apartment and clean up because she kept the apartment messy and didn't clean up, so I used to do it for her. I was doing anything that I could to win her back. Including looking like a dummy.

After a few months as I predicted, she wanted to come back, but I didn't let her. I said we could be friends. I wanted to make her feel how I felt when she left me. Since I had all this free time I decided to go back to school and get a degree in something. I can't even remember what I chose but I can tell you that the school I chose isn't even open anymore so I'm kind of glad that I didn't even finish there.

I was doing data entry for a cabinet company making $8.10 per hour. I remember that dollar amount because when I first started, I was only making $8 an hour. Then a year later for the review I got a .10 cent raise. I didn't know anything about being grateful back then. I was actually offended. I wasn't getting any assistance of any kind. No welfare, no child support, nothing.

Yeah, I was working but I hated that job and the people there. My second child's father ended up working there too. I helped him get a job there. We rarely saw each other though because he worked in the warehouse and the manager didn't want the warehouse workers in the office. The office was full of women. The manager was a chauvinist.

By this time two years had passed, and my 2nd child's father and I began talking again. He lived around the corner from where I lived so we agreed to co-parent. He would get the baby for a week, and I would get the baby the following week. It actually worked out well. He moved on and was dating again and so did I. Every now and again he would ask could he come over and eat my pussy so he could be in practice, and I sure did let him. We did not have sexual intercourse though because I knew if we did, he would want me back. I'm not being conceited when I say this but keep in mind, I was his first everything. I did not want to him to drum up any feelings for me and think we were going to get back together because we were not. If I didn't know anything, I knew that I did not want to be married to him or any man. We had a mutual understanding, that is all. On holidays, I would go over to his apartment with the baby and cook meals and we would eat together. He would let me come over to his apartment and wash our clothes because my apartment didn't have a washer and dryer inside and I had a 2-year-old. I ended up serving him with divorce papers. He was supposed to sign and turn it in. I paid for everything. I wasn't expecting him to pay for anything. I just wanted him to sign it and turn it in. The divorce never happened. We'll talk about that later.

At the time I knew where my heart was, and it was with my first girlfriend. I wanted her back. She at the time didn't want me back, so I went back to what I knew. I thought I would do better by being with a man, so I started a sexual relationship that was forbidden because he was married. I don't like men. I found myself going back to doing things that I was not happy doing because I did not have what I wanted in my life. I was settling yet again.

This time we had an understanding that this was just sex, and it wasn't gonna be anything more. It was exciting because I was fucking someone that she mentioned she wanted in the past. This was my payback to her. At the same time, I met this guy at a club, and I thought that we were going to have a sexual relationship. We had sex one time, and I was not impressed so I ignored him. He used to call my phone and pop up at my house and I would just be looking at him from the balcony. Slowly but surely, he got the message that I wasn't into him. I don't know what it was about me that I could not bring myself to turn someone down or to tell them how I really felt. Don't judge me.

Around that time, it was 2003. My mom called and asked me to move back to Beaumont. She needed help with the bills because her baby daddy went to prison. She couldn't afford to pay the bills by herself. I feel like all of this was me getting my karma back for how I treated my youngest daughter's father. I took it. I didn't take it hard though. I moved back to Beaumont to help my mama. I quit school, packed my stuff and moved on back home for two years. My mom did surprise me though because when I came back to Beaumont, she bought me a computer and a fax machine and got me my own landline so that I could continue going to school. I ended up enrolling in another school to get my bachelor's degree.

After I moved back to Beaumont, I found a job at a call center, and I worked there for about two years. See, that number two again? I started another sexual relationship with someone who I worked with. He didn't know the situation that was going on and he didn't care because he had his own situation going on. We agreed to keep it quiet and have no feelings involved. This went on for a few months.

I did not hear from baby daddy #2 after I moved back to Beaumont. I didn't receive no calls, no visits or no checks. He disappeared and I was not trying to contact him. I went ahead and filed child support on him just like I did with the other baby daddy. For years I didn't get a thing out of either one of them but more on that later.

When it came to coming out as being a lesbian, I was actually forced to come out because somebody outed me. I told my best friend that me and this girl were together. She told her brother, and he told the world, and it got back to my sister. My sister was fighting people in the street behind it because I hadn't come out yet. She was literally fighting with people to defend my name.

So, I ended up coming out. I came out to my daddy first. I always go to my dad first, just because I will say however he reacts, that's going to tell me how everybody else would react. I thought my dad would be upset. However, when I told him, he said, "Okay, and?" I was shocked and I said, "Did you hear what I said?" He told me that there was nothing wrong with it. I told my mom I had something to tell her, and she said, "I already know, and I love you anyway." I was like, oh, shit this is going to be easy. They were the only people I actually felt like I wanted to tell so if anybody else ever found out that's how they found out.

When my first girlfriend and I talked about coming out I was afraid that my parents wouldn't be accepting and she was excited because she said her family wasn't like that, boy was she wrong. When she came out to her family and told them that she was with me, they all lost it. I was called all kind of names in the book. I was accused of turning their baby out. I laughed on the inside because she turned me out, I had never been with a woman before, she had. And now that I think about it, she did not defend me she let them say all kind of things about me in front of me and did not speak up for me. I did not speak up for myself either.

I moved back to Beaumont to help my mama, so I was back living with my mom. By this time, I have two kids. So, I found a job and I was helping her pay the bills. I stayed there for about three months before I had to get the fuck away. My mama thought I was her man and babysitter. She was trying to take all my lil paycheck and would just up and leave my baby sister with me.

Eventually, my ex moved to Beaumont too. I used to go to Houston every weekend because that's how much I hated Beaumont. I worked Monday through Friday. On Fridays when I got off, I took my ass to Houston to see my ex. No, I didn't take the kids with me. I left them with my mama.

I would go out there to see her because I missed her, and I missed being in Houston. We still had a friendship. One day when I was leaving from my weekend visit with her, she started crying and said she wanted to be with me. She said that she wanted to come with me to Beaumont. I was like, damn, I ain't never had no broad crying over me. That actually made me feel special at the time because I didn't think anybody would care enough about me to cry over me except my child's father, but I didn't count him because I didn't want him.

I said OK, I'll give it another shot. I packed her up and moved her to Beaumont. I found us a house and at first, I told her she didn't have to work. When the bills started coming in, I told her, "Oh, no. Bae you gotta work." I ended up getting her a job where I worked. We were in different departments, and everything was fine. We were out there for two years. We had a house, and we were raising the kids. Around this time, she befriended this woman from work. I didn't care, because I was happy. You know, I had my girl and I have my kids, and everything was great. We were a happy family, or so I thought.

I suddenly got this feeling that something was not right. She was starting to spend more and more time away from home outside of work. One night, she told me she was going to get her car washed. However, it was pitch black in Beaumont and no car wash stayed open that late. Nobody would honestly be washing their car that late at night. I told my friend to come and ride with me to find her car. Beaumont was small, so we were able to ride around, and we found her car parked at her co-worker's house. The co-worker happened to be an in-law of someone I know. This same person tried to talk to me, and I turned her down.

We sat there for a while because I was hoping that she would come out and come home. She didn't. I was hoping to see a light on or a flicker of a TV through the apartment window. There wasn't. A windstorm of emotions filled me. I was ashamed, mad, scared, hurt, & relieved all at the same time. I was ashamed because I had my friend with me who warned me that this was happening, and I didn't want to listen. I was mad because my friend was right.

Eventually I told my friend to go ahead and bring me home. Where we lived, we use the back door as the main entrance so I thought I would just wait for her to come in and talk to her. I think reality hit me when she came in through the front door. She never used the front door. we never used the front door. I don't know what came over me, but I stood behind the front door waiting for her to come inside. It was pitch dark and I promise all I intended to do was talk to her, but in the heat of the moment just started swinging. I never put my hands on anyone before. And I don't condone doing it at that time. I lost control of myself and next thing I know we were fighting. I told her she lied to me she's a liar and why was she doing this to me and why was she doing this to our family. I'll tell her that I was in love with her which I was at the time. You couldn't tell me nothing bad about her. She was the epitome of I'll drink her bath water.

She told me that she didn't love me like that, and she just wanted to be friends. Friends? I didn't wanna be friends I wanted to marry this girl I wanted to give her the life that I thought she deserved at the time. When she told me that she didn't love me like that she might as well had shot me in the heart. When I heard those words, I lost it. Then she moved upstairs when she used to sleep with me in our bedroom.

I thought at the time that I could be friends, but how can I be friends with someone that I was in love with as she was dating someone else, and we all worked together? Damn how could she cheat on me with somebody we worked with? How could she cheat on me period? When I went back to work that Monday, I swear everybody knew what happened. I don't know if it was me being paranoid, but I felt like everyone knew what happened and they were staring at me in awe and shock. To make it even worse she started sitting with the person that she was cheating on me with. I felt like the stupidest Fool. Even after this I still tried to get her to stay with me. I was so distraught. I remember that I used to go to my car on my lunch break and cry. I was so depressed that I lost 50 pounds in three months. During that time all I did was drink alcohol and cry and listen to sad music that made me feel even worse. Emancipation of MiMi was the CD I ran into the ground during this breakup. I definitely was self-loathing and punishing myself.

She started letting the person sleep at the house that we shared. That I paid majority of the bills in. They would be upstairs having a great time and I would try my best to move on. I didn't have it in me to kick both of their assess and put them out. To keep from going to the house I worked all the overtime that I could because I could not bear to see, hear, or know that she was loving on someone else when she was only supposed to be loving on me. I was finally doing right by someone.

I went from being broken hearted to pissed the fuck off. I ended up letting one of my friends I worked with know what was going on and he felt so sorry for me. He ended up catching a recording of my ex being rude to a customer. He asked me if I wanted him to report it. I was hurt so, I wanted her to hurt too so I told him yes and that call got her fired. I kind of felt bad but at the same time that was a little bit of relief for me because I didn't have to see them booed up at the job anymore as if I wasn't there as if we weren't in a long-term relationship. I just got to see it at home.

For some reason I thought that would make her want to move out and go be with her new girlfriend, but no she stayed at the house unbothered. I was the only one that was bothered. Actually, I was dying inside. I tried to move on so quickly that for half a second, I thought about dating men again. I actually tried to date a man again but that quickly left my mind because I was not attracted to men. I wanted to be with a woman. I was done lying to myself and hurting others in the process. What happened in that relationship I chalked it up as being my karma for what I did in my relationship with my second child's father.

I ended up signing up for a chat account where I would eventually meet my second girlfriend. She was nice and accepting of my two kids and she lived in Houston, where I wanted to be in the first place. And I found myself doing what I did before, getting into a relationship when I was not ready and moving in with her just to get out of Beaumont. This time I really loved her, and I was not using her. She was so sweet to me and the kids in the beginning it was almost too good to be true. I think I ignored the red flags all because I wanted to be in a relationship with someone who not only told me they love me but showed me as well and she did that, at first.

When we met, she let me know that she recently moved to Houston from Austin. She was originally from up north. Initially she told me she had moved to Texas because of school but later on in the relationship I found out that she moved for a girl. Apparently, this is something people do, move from state to state to be with other people. I wasn't judging I just had never done it before. the farthest I had gone for someone is hour and a half away from home definitely not to another state. As many times as I had thought about it, I was too chicken shit to move to another state and be away from people that I knew.

When we first got together, and we were all moved in she had some leftover baggage from a previous relationship. I told her that she needed to clear that up so that she can move on with me apparently, she owed this person money for her phone bill. I ended up paying off her debt so the girl could leave her alone.

Everything was great between us. We were a happy family. We were eating at the table as a family I just knew that I had my Cosby show family. We went around the table and talked about our day we shared we did things together we had family time I was very happy. I was so happy that I ended up buying her a vehicle because I didn't want her riding the bus to work anymore. I thought we had a future together so I was doing what I could to help her level up.

I also thought my kids were happy. I fostered a relationship to where I let my children know that if they had any issue no matter what it was that they could come and talk to me about it. This is something that I did not have so I wanted to make sure that my children had it I wanted to make sure that they trusted me with their secrets or with their issues. As much as I reiterated to them that they could talk to me unfortunately they did not. At least not about everything.

During this relationship I started having behavioral issues with my first baby. I wasn't used to her acting out, so I didn't know what to do I did what I thought I was supposed to which was reach out to my mom and dad. They were no help. Every time I would try to go to them to seek guidance, they will blame me for whatever issue was going on. I know I was the adult in this situation, but I did not know how to handle behavioral issues from a kid who didn't used to act bad.

At the time she was not getting along with my second girlfriend. I let my second girlfriend verbally discipline my children, never physically. I will admit that my children were spoiled by me and by the time I noticed it was too late to reel them back in. This was a period in which I was trying to show my oldest baby the value of money and how nothing was going to ever get handed to her and that she had to work for anything that she wanted. I guess I didn't do it right.

That relationship lasted 2 years. I was beginning to think that the number two was my number regarding all things. Two kids. Two baby daddies. Two girlfriends. Both cheated on me. Any job that I was at I only lasted two years. Going into our second year, I started having issues with my youngest child. These were behavioral issues. The teacher would call to talk to me about thing she was saying and doing in class at the time I thought she was just a little kid that's doing little kids stuff it wasn't that big of a deal until once she got in trouble at home and her punishment was that she couldn't go on a field trip. She took it upon herself to fill out the permission slip and try to turn it in herself the teacher called me and tell me about it and that's all her know that she could not go on this field trip, and she didn't. This is the start of the behavioral issues I'll talk more about that later.

So, my girlfriend at the time started talking to an old friend. This old friend ended up being someone who they had mutual feelings for but for whatever reason they were never together. I was fine with it until one day we were on a trip to Las Vegas, and she excused herself to go downstairs and was gone over an hour.

the person who came with us came and told me that she was downstairs talking on the phone to some girl, and did I know who she was talking to; of course, I did not know. I should have headed that red flag too, but I did not.

LIFE CHALLENGES

That incident was maybe six months into our relationship so I didn't really pay it any mind. Then, I noticed her on the phone more than normal. I remember one day she came to me and said, "I'm buying her some books for her for class, and I could do what I want with my money." That was a damn red flag right there. I just said, "OK" and kept it going.

Like I said before I wanted us to grow together both personally and professionally. She was working in a warehouse and wasn't making much money. I was an administrative assistant, and I was making decent money. I encouraged her to seek other jobs that pay more because I saw her worth more than she did. Eventually she listened to me and began looking for other jobs and finally landed a great job with a major distributor. She was a delivery driver. I was so happy, and she was too. This was going to be the beginning of us building our empire, or so I thought. Once she became comfortable in her new position, she became too comfortable with the change and the status that she was being given.

Other women were starting to notice her because I changed her style. I changed the way she dressed. I chose her clothes. And no, I'm not just saying that. This is facts. She used to dress like an old man and had a haircut like one too. I encouraged her to get that haircut to something more relevant and she started looking better not that she looked bad in the beginning, but you can tell when someone has been upgraded and she was. The thing is she was letting those compliments from randoms go to her head. We were starting to hang out with other couples and doing things socially. It ended up being every weekend thing and I was growing tired of it and little did I know at the time the couples that we were hanging out with was growing tired of us.

One event that sticks out in my mind is there was going to be a birthday celebration dinner for one of the people in the social circle. I had a funny feeling about going and I told her we were not invited because we weren't. She insisted that we were invited and that we should go so I followed her lead reluctantly and went and as I stated we were not invited because when we got there, they were looking at us like *what the fuck are y'all doing here?* I was humiliated. I felt the vibes and ended up leaving.

I didn't understand why we were the hated couple until later. I found out that my significant other was stirring up mess and I was guilty by association of course. In the lesbian world if your partner is doing something bad, even if you're not doing it too, you are doing it because that's your partner so when one goes the other must go to. Lesson learned.

A few months later she started going out without me. I didn't mind I wanted her to have her free time. I was in school, and I had my kids so that's where my focus was. I never wanted anyone who was with me to feel like I was a ball and chain hence my last relationship. I remember she came home and told me that she had met someone. I didn't care. I have never been the jealous type, so it didn't bother me that she had new friends.

Instead of going out physically and being social I found myself on chat lines just having casual conversation with other lesbians because I did not know any. I actually ran across someone I knew from my hometown. We started casually having conversation and then we took it offline I started texting and talking on the phone it was cool I was happy to have a friend.

On September 15th, 2007, I received my bachelor's degree in business management. It was an exciting time for me. My family came out and supported me. This was one of the only times that I was really happy. After graduation I immediately applied to enter the masters program. I definitely had something to prove to myself.

Eventually I would introduce my girlfriend to my new friend, and we all got acquainted. We even entertained the thought of being Poly. If you don't know what that is, it's basically a three-way relationship amongst consensual adults. It didn't go far at all actually I think it ended before it began. My girlfriend and this girl were hitting it off too well and I felt like they were leaving me out and I did not like that. I thought I was being an adult by addressing my issue with each person. I never was really good at communicating verbally, so I would write letters and that's what I did I wrote a whole e-mail to my friend explaining to her how I felt and why I felt the way I was feeling. She in turn replied and said that ain't her problem I need to talk to my girlfriend. So that told me right there she wasn't a friend.

We ended up still hanging out, but you can tell that the vibe had changed. My friend loved her shoes, and she asked me to start helping her dress better. I was flattered because I wanted to be a stylist and had previously mentioned that to her. I was like oh she could be my first client and I could show her off and eventually I will be able to dress celebrities. It made me feel good to know that someone was entrusting me with their fashion. However, this never happened.

To put the nail in the coffin my girlfriend sent our friend a beautiful bouquet of flowers. I didn't mind. What I did mind is that my girlfriend gave me some little raggedy flowers as an afterthought so I wouldn't get mad at her giving the beautiful bouquet to my friend. I know this because that's what she told me. This triggered me and caused me to not like flowers and to this day I do not like people sending me flowers.

I can't remember exactly how me, and my friend's relationship ended but it did end. Thinking back, I can say that my ex played a major part in why I lost my friend. I didn't realize how messy she was. She would literally go back and repeat things that I told her in confidence. She made the almost Poly relationship into a competition when it shouldn't have been. All I know is that it got to where me and my friend were not talking, and she even started saying mean things about me. I never said anything mean about her, but you never know what my ex told her. One thing in particular that I remember her saying is that I couldn't dress. And all I thought to myself was if I couldn't dress why were you asking me to dress you? People just be saying shit, so I let her be and we had no more communication. She did stay in touch with my ex though.

The next instance that occurred was my ex started talking frequently with the old friend who she was talking to while we were on our vacation in Vegas. I tried not to be suspicious I guess I was just ignoring my guts which was telling me something was going on. The first car that my ex had gave out on her, so her uncle who lived in another state told her that he had a car she would just have to come and get it. She made that her opportunity to not only go and get the car that I gave her the money for, but she also made a pit stop and paid a visit to the out-of-town friend. It wasn't a secret. I knew where she was going. I was just too weak to tell her not to go see another woman just go and get the car and come home. All the while my stomach was churning because I knew this wasn't right, but I was accepting it. So, I basically paid for my girlfriend to go see another woman and to go pick up a vehicle. Karma turned around quickly because when she was out there with the other woman, they had car trouble, and she was about to miss her plane to go and get the car. She called me asking for money and my dumb ass sent it to her. My thoughts at the time were that I didn't want her to lose her job because she did have to come back home. I did not want her stranded.

She eventually made it to the state where she was picking up the car, it turned out to be a truck. She was able to drive it all the way home and then the truck stopped working! We ended up having to push it across the street to the mechanic shop. Then we found out that there was a mechanic's lien on the truck. And to top it off, it was thousands of dollars to truck fixed, so we were down to one car. We decided not to invest any money into this truck because one it cost too much and two it had a mechanic's lien on it. Her uncle failed to tell her that part before she took the car, so we ended up leaving it at the mechanic shop and who knows what happened to it after that.

I did not know whether to be mad at her or mad at myself for being a dummy. Hell, I thought I was in love, and I thought you were supposed to do whatever you needed to do for your partner to make them happy. Since we were down to one car and she had to be to work for 4:00 o'clock in the morning, I had to get up and bring her. I think we did this for about 6 weeks, and then I bought her another truck. So now I'm sure you're asking where I got all this money from. I was in school, and I was using my financial aid checks to purchase vehicles for her.

A few months later comes this friend that I don't know where she came from. Apparently, she had met someone younger with no kids who she found interesting. She swore to me that they were friends only and my dumb ass believed her. They went from texting to talking, to going out, to exchanging emails; and while all of this was happening, I was withdrawing. Eventually, I built my wall up and I shut down.

What led to our breakup was my ex went out for the evening and I knew she was going to be with this female. I also knew that they would have sex. She didn't tell me this, but I felt it, I knew it. It was the same feeling I had before. Sure, enough she came home late one night but she had her underclothes on. She got in our bed, and I smelled the scent of the other woman's pussy on my ex. Before I knew it, I had taken both of my feet and pushed my ex out of the bed and told her to get her ass on the couch. How dare she climb in our bed after having sex with another bitch and then not even bother to wash up. A woman knows another woman's scent and the scent that I smelled wasn't mine because we stopped having sex. After this, we really stopped having sex. I found out that she came home and took her clothes off downstairs and threw them in the washing machine I washed all our clothes so she thought she would sneak them in, and I would not see or smell another woman's pussy.

We both came to the agreement that it was time for her to move out. After two weeks on the couch, she found herself an apartment down the street. The idea was that we were going to take some time apart and get back together eventually after we were done working on ourselves. I really wanted to be with her. I imagined our wedding. I imagined us being together, but I did not imagine us growing old together. That right there should have told me something, but again this is me and it didn't.

Keep in mind that I still had two children and a job, and I was still in school, even though I had this job I could not afford the town home that we were living in. I refused to uproot my children from what they were used to, so I ended up getting a second job. I wanted so badly to not be like my mother. We moved from place to place to place and I went from school to school to school and I did not want that for my children because I remember how I felt. I ended up finding a part time job in the evenings maybe two or three nights a week. I still worked a full-time job during the day, so I relied on my oldest child to watch my youngest while I was out. I would always make sure that they had dinner, and I was home no later than 10 thirty 11:00 o'clock PM. Yes, I was tired, but it was worth it because we stayed in that beautiful town home for 10 years and my children knew what stability was.

It was June 2008 when I decided that I no longer wanted to work on my relationship with my ex-girlfriend. My first ex-girlfriend and I were friends, but I could not be friends with my second ex-girlfriend even though I tried. I had maybe a few weeks of being single when I began to get bored. I was tired of working and coming home working and coming home and not having a social life. My children were fine they were fed they were clothed they had extracurricular activities, but I had nothing and no one for myself. Some may call that a sacrifice, but I called it a punishment and I wasn't having it.

To solidify the fact that I was single yet again after a bad breakup of being cheated on I went to my favorite ice cream parlor bought a gallon of ice cream and ate it over the course of a weekend. I definitely wasn't going to do what I did the last time I had a breakup which was starve and only drink alcohol and worked to death. I also did not want my children to see me upset, so I would send them to my aunt's house to play with their cousins and go to church. This was my way of having me time and their way of bonding with their cousins.

As I look back, I now realize that my oldest daughter's behavior got better after I broke up with my second ex. To this day, I never asked her why she didn't like her or why she was acting the way she did. But I do know that after me and my second ex broke up, my oldest baby tried to plea with me to get back with my ex. I don't know what that was about, but I had to show her that we don't go backwards. And just because someone apologizes for their wrongdoing doesn't mean that we should take them back.

In June of 2008, I created a profile on this website so that I could look around for someone to play with. I was broken up from my second ex-girlfriend I didn't have any male friend entertainers because I had decided once and for all that I was done with that. No more going backwards, even if it was temporary. I was back to not having any friends. I was feeling alone. I didn't have anyone to talk to that would understand what I was going through.

I ended up befriending maybe 3 women from the website, one of which became one of my closest friends, one I didn't even start dating because of her background. When I say background, I mean that I did not want to be with someone who was known in the streets. What I mean by that is I did not want to be with someone that everybody knew especially in the "Lesbian World" damn sure not in the lesbian world because it is so small. (Yes, we do have our own world.) Me and that person talked on the phone and that's about it. The last person that I met sent me this e-mail and it was very intriguing that it made me look at her profile.

From her profile I immediately judged her and thought to myself, "Oh my God she is ghetto." I started looking some more at her pictures and thought, "Yeah, she's broke." I kept looking some more and saw that she was a kid. When I say kid, I mean she was 23 and I was 32. I'm thinking to myself, "What the hell am I going to do with a 23-year-old?" Then the light bulb came on, "I'm gonna fuck her." I'm sure this young girl isn't going to want any commitment and at the time I damn sure didn't want one either. I waited a couple of days before I replied to her e-mail.

Chapter 6

I'LL MAKE IT THROUGH

It was the end of the school year by now and my oldest was 16 years old and the youngest was six years old. I really needed a break from them. I was in one of those moods where I just did not like to interact with them because they were both in these weird stages and I didn't want to deal with it, but I had to because I'm their mom. In my mind I knew I needed to talk to someone but also in my mind I kept telling myself that I couldn't afford it. I knew that talking to my family or friends was not an option as I had already tried it and they did not hear me.

I was still mourning the breakup of my second ex. I still loved her, but I was not in love with her. By this time, she had stopped going out of her way to make me happy. I started feeling like she took me for granted and I was devastated that she cheated on me. My self-esteem was at an all-time low.

I was so frustrated that it was ridiculous! My patience was nonexistent. I was so unhappy I couldn't even hide it. I knew what was wrong I just did not want to admit it. I felt overwhelmed and I felt like I was being used. I didn't like that feeling that I was having. I was trying not to cry because during this time it was around Father's Day and my youngest was on the phone with her dad. I was pissed off that she made this big ass card for him for Father's Day. I was angry because he didn't do shit for her. He didn't provide financial support. He did not come and get her and spend time with her. He barely called her. Any time they spoke on the phone it was because she asked me to call him. I hated the fact that she loved a man so much who didn't do anything for her. One thing I always knew is that I would never deny my children access to their fathers. I never spoke ill about either one of them even though I had my own personal thoughts about how shit went down. I never shared this with the kids. I always said to myself that they would see in the end for themselves what kind of people their dads were.

I wanted to run away and not come back. I thought several times about just disappearing. My temporary getaway was me going to the corner store and buying Al Capones. (Al Capones are cigarillos dipped in rum.) Then, going to the park and smoking about three or four of them and then I would go home. That's what I did to relax myself. I was so unhappy, and I did not know what would make me happy. At this point in my life, I just needed a support system I needed someone that I could talk to and not be judged or criticized. I needed to not be told what to do or that it was my fault. I did not have that, so I kept all of my thoughts and feelings inside which wasn't good.

After the breakup with my second ex, I felt like I wasn't good enough for anyone. I wanted to understand her so badly. I knew I loved her because I was hurting. If I didn't love her and want to be with her, I wouldn't have been wasting my time writing about it and in my feelings about it. I was having terrible issues with my body image because my second ex left me for someone younger and smaller. She made sure I knew that. She wasn't better looking than me though. After that happened, I felt like I wasn't pretty enough, I wasn't fine enough, I wasn't sexy enough. (This was before Keisha Cole 'I Should Have Cheated' came out).

I just couldn't help but feel like something was missing inside of me. I didn't know what it was, but I just knew I wasn't happy. I think I was trying too hard to be happy with my second ex. I was even talking to my first ex about it. I became so insecure & doubting myself, questioning myself, and I never used to do that.

The last thing my second ex said to me was, "Do you think God is still punishing you for what you did in the past?" Past meaning all the things I had did before I met her, she knew about it. Needless to say, June of 2008 was a very long month.

I know one thing, the passive Shawnti got put on hold. I was tired of being run over and tired of playing nice. I was tired of giving and tired of being a savior to people who run over me and treat me like shit. I know my worth, I know I'm a good woman. I know I'll be a good woman to someone who deserves me. No more settling for close enough. I just have to accept that it will take longer for me to get exactly what I want. I can wait. I know that I'm definitely worth more than I allow myself. I know I'm not perfect, therefore I'm not looking for perfection in someone else. I have my flaws that I am working on. But my good outweighs my bad. And I want that in someone: the good outweighs their bad.

The 23-year-old whose e-mail I decided to respond to, we began talking casually. She would come over and spend the evening just talking, eating and watching TV; nothing sexual & while the children were not home. I did not want my kids to meet her because this was only supposed to be casual so there was no need. At this point we were just enjoying each other's company. I was heavy into *Girlfriends* the TV show, so I had adopted Joan's '90-day rule' of no sex when I'm dating someone. More on that & her later.

Before I knew it, summer '08 was over and the kids were back home and ready to start school. I had one going to the 9th grade and another starting kindergarten. We had gone school shopping like we always did, they were ready. I was in school obtaining my Master's degree, working a full-time job, and working a part time job. The kids were going to church on Sundays with my aunt and her kids. I didn't like that shit, so I was looking for one for me to go to myself. I had gotten a rhythm down and everything was going well.

A few months have passed, and my friend finally was introduced to my children. They both seemed excited to meet her. I don't know if she was excited to meet them or not. I couldn't read her face. Around September, my friend was beginning to point out things about my children and I did not agree with at first. I used to put my children up on pedestals and believe that they could do no wrong, but boy was I wrong. I had rose colored glasses on when it came to my children, but as the years went on, I found out that I was the delusional one and I quickly took those rose-colored glasses off when it came to them.

I was a single mother working two jobs. I felt bad leaving the kids at home, although I didn't work the second job every day, I still didn't want them to be latchkey kids. My oldest daughter started looking at boys, so that was an issue for me; especially when I was not home to supervise. I was close to getting my

Master's degree. I was excited about finally being able to take care of my family and maintain the lifestyle that we had gotten used to.

All throughout my oldest daughter school years up until 9th grade she was an honor student. I rarely had any problems out of her (before & after my 2nd ex) she was my good girl. That is until she entered high school and she started noticing boys and apparently boys started noticing her. That was a big issue for me because I did not want her to follow in my footsteps and be a teen mom. I kind of figured that I had lost her when her grades started slipping. I did everything I possibly could to keep her busy or occupied so that she didn't have enough free time to be in someone else's face. But as we all know, where there is a will there is a way and that was a battle that I could not win.

My youngest daughter was entering kindergarten and I was excited about that because I remember how exciting kindergarten was for me and how I was excited about my oldest daughter going to kindergarten too. Believe me when I tell you those three experiences were totally different.

Back to my oldest daughter, like I said she was having wide eyes for little boys which is understandable at that age, so I felt like it was important that I talked to her about having sex and the consequences of it. I wanted to make sure that she understood that if she decided to start having sex that she needed to be responsible. I was not condoning her having sex before marriage or at the age of 16, but I wanted her to be prepared. I wanted her to be educated on every aspect because I was not. Needless to say, it went in one ear and out the other. I'll just leave it at that for now.

So, during this time I was still working and raising the children and going to school. My oldest daughter was so boy crazy that it was ridiculous. She defied me at every chance just to be in this one little boy in particular face. My youngest one was getting in trouble it seemed like every other day at school for talking out of turn or for doing things she wasn't supposed to be doing. It started to become a lot. I was glad that the holidays were coming up so there would be breaks.

During the holiday break my oldest daughter wanted to go to my aunt's house with all the kids which was fine. By this time my youngest baby's dad call me and ask could he start coming to get his daughter and of course I say yes because like I said earlier, I never denied him the right to be with his child; he just chose not to be. When he came to get her for the holiday break that was the first time we had seen each other in years. That was also the first time that he saw his only child in years since I had moved back to Beaumont.

I asked him what happened to the divorce papers because I was under the impression that the divorce was final. I've never been divorced before, so I didn't know how the process worked and I didn't ask anybody. He let me know that he signed the papers and gave it to his mom to mail off. I just said OK and left it at that. Later, I made the decision to go ahead and file child support on him as he was not holding up his end of the bargain and not helping out. The only thing I ever asked him for was help with school clothes and school supplies. I never bothered him in between that time, and he couldn't even do that.

I brought my friend with me over the break because she did not have family here in the city. At that time, I was big on family and loved to be around my family. My grandfather was still alive, and we used to gather at his house like we used to when my grandmother was alive. I was very surprised that my family was receptive to her. This would have been the third person I brought around my family, but this time was different. She ended up having a good time and I enjoyed her being around so much that after that, she never went back home.

This was the around the time I said ok, well it's time for my kids to meet her and it's time for her kid to meet me. Yes, she had a daughter as well that was two years younger that my youngest. I didn't mind though because she was young and how could I say I don't wanna date someone with kids and I have them. My friend did tell me though that she usually didn't date women with kids, but she had the choice to either leave or stay and she chose to stay.

As I stated before I was having behavioral issues with my second child. There was a period where she was great at home and I had no issues out of her, but the teacher was always calling or emailing me about her behavior in class. Most of her behavior at school was centered around sex. When I say that I mean that she was writing inappropriate words or sending notes that were not appropriate to boys or writing down song lyrics that were inappropriate for her age. I was letting her listen to the radio but after so many instances I stopped allowing radio other than gospel. I also began monitoring what she was watching on TV when she was with me. Unfortunately, although I reached out to anyone who would take her for the weekend or what have you, I let them know what I was experiencing and how I was trying to combat it and if they would also do the same. I wasn't trying to control anyone or how they do things that was not my intention I just wanted help. I didn't get it.

Suddenly out of nowhere (to me) at home she would lie about any little thing that didn't need to be lied about. I didn't understand why she was lying so much. I thought it was because she was just at that age, but it was way worse than that. It started to bother me. I thought maybe if I spent more time with her that she would get better. Sometimes I would keep her home from school so we could have a girl's day. Sometimes I would take her out to eat. I even started going up to her school and having lunch with her once a week. I know she enjoyed these things, but I think she enjoyed them for the wrong reasons. I say this because especially for school since none of the other parents would come and do the things that I was doing. Her teachers would commend me and tell me to keep up the good work. As an observation I feel like she liked me being there to make the other kids jealous because their mom or dad wasn't coming to eat lunch with them. That didn't stop me from doing what I was doing though. I was just trying to show her that I love her and cared about her.

Since she was my last child, I just knew that this time I could get it right. I was doing all of the things that I wanted done to me and for me when I was her age. My mom never came up to the school for anything good for me. She came up to the school when I was acting bad. My mom never took me out to eat or spent time with me just me and her. I imagine that me and my youngest child would have this unbreakable bond and that was my goal to make that happen. However, it did not work out that way.

There was a period where her hair was beginning to fall out and I thought maybe it was because of the perms that I was putting in her hair. I tried getting her braids so that she could go natural. I was going to stop putting perms in, but the braids were falling out of her head too and I didn't know what was going on, so I decided to cut the perm out of her head and start over. I'd try a different product to get her hair growing again, and it was growing. I had begun putting twists in her hair. I would wash her hair and condition it every two weeks and retwist it every two weeks faithfully in hopes that it would keep growing and get healthier and fuller. I'll let you know why I'm saying this later on in the book.

Remember the field trip incident with my youngest daughter that I mentioned earlier? This was the beginning of the noticeable behavioral issues that we were experiencing with my youngest child. After the field trip incident, it literally seemed like every week the teacher was calling me about something that my youngest was doing. It was simple stuff like not following directions talking in class, things like that and I did not take those too seriously because I thought to myself that she was in kindergarten that's what five- and six-year-olds do. She was being good at home, so I wasn't too hard on her about her behavior at the time. But then she started acting out at home too. It started off with lies, again something the kindergartener would do. Then there was her tormenting her older sister, again something a little sister does. The punishments where you know go to your room, no TV, a spanking or stand in the corner, things like that. I never could have imagined that this was the beginning of years of disciplinary issues and essentially a family disconnect.

We lived in a three-bedroom 3-bathroom townhome and all of the bedrooms were upstairs. There was one instance where we all were upstairs, and someone knocked on the door. The youngest one, 6 at the time, took it upon herself to answer the door which she knew was a no-no. She answered the door because she knew who it was. There was a small window on the side of the door where you could peep to see who was outside. It was a little girl from across the way and apparently, she came to ask could she borrow one of our DVD's and the youngest one gave it to her without my permission.

When I found out what happened and why she did it, I spanked her. I spanked her on her butt for 1: answering the door when she already knew she was not allowed to do so and 2: giving our property to someone without my permission. The next day was school, and I received a phone call from CPS (Child Protective Services) stating that I needed to go to the CPS office because I was being investigated for child abuse. Apparently, the youngest child went to her teacher and told on me and said that I whipped her, which I did.

I had nothing to hide however, I had never been called to a CPS office to be investigated, so I asked my new friend to come with me just in case because I didn't know what to expect. I left work early and my current friend and I went to the CPS office to see what this was about because I had no clue. When I got there, I was met by an officer, and I wanted my friend to come in the room with me, but they said that she could not and that was fine. I just wanted her there for security, but as long as she was in the building, I was fine.

I remember going into this office sitting in a chair and waiting for someone to come and talk to me. Finally, a lady came in the office and sat down and introduced herself and she let me know that a teacher from my second baby's school called CPS for child abuse. The lady asked me what happened, and I told her the story about her opening the door and giving the DVD without my permission. The lady agreed that she would have done the same thing however, me spanking my youngest left my handprint on her backside which is why the teacher called CPS. So, in my mind I'm thinking this little girl pulled down her pants and showed this white lady her ass.

The CPS lady said that it was OK to spank her, but I may have done it too hard which is why there was a mark on her behind. She then proceeds to pull out this diagram of the back of a naked child. She drew a circle around where the handprint was on my youngest daughter. I didn't know I hit her that hard. I did feel bad afterwards. The CPS lady proceeded to show me the proper way to spank my child which is no more than three taps with my open bare hand on her bottom. I just watched and shook my head as if I understood so that I could get out of there.

No charges were filed on me, and the case was dismissed. As I stated before, I didn't realize I spanked her that hard to where I left a handprint. I would never do anything to hurt my children like that. That didn't mean I was gonna stop spanking them though, because I didn't.

Later that day when the kids came home, I did talk to my youngest daughter and let her know that her telling the teacher that I spanked her was not gonna stop me from spanking her. I told her I shouldn't have hit her that hard that she did deserve to be disciplined. I let her know that anytime she does something wrong, depending on what it is, she will be corrected for it. Apparently, my youngest child did not like that conversation because things got a whole lot worse afterwards.

My friend who went with me also let me know that I didn't do anything wrong and suggested maybe next time, if the occasion calls for it, make sure she has clothes on so that she won't have any marks. Again, I wasn't trying to mark up my child I was just disciplining her for doing something she had no business doing.

Chapter EIGHT

JUST LET ME LIVE AND BE HAPPY

As life is going on my friend and I are getting to know each other a little more and everything was cool. At the same time, my 2nd ex was trying to get back with me, but that was not a chance I was willing to take. She had announced to me that she wanted to get back with me and she was going to do whatever it took to get me back. What she didn't know is that it wasn't how she got me, it's how she should've kept me. It wasn't hard for her to get me in the beginning, but like I said, the things that I wanted her to do she wasn't willing to do. I refused to go through another summer of her listening to random bitches and then deciding that a family was too much for her.

I just wanted to love someone and have them love me back. I knew that I had people in my corner but what I'm saying is that I want to have someone so in love with me just to love me the way that I want and need to be loved. There was a point where I was feeling lonely and that made me think that I prefer to have somebody with me. I did not like to be single. It wasn't that I couldn't be single because I know I can, I just wanted to be in a relationship with a giver as I am a giver. Then I want to know that I am loving someone the way that they want and need to be loved I wanted this to be reciprocated, not one sided like it was in my last relationship. In my opinion I gave her everything that she needed even though I didn't agree with half of what she did and said, I supported her. What I can say is that I was a people pleaser. I felt like for all that I did for her she didn't do enough for me. Then it made me think was I just never satisfied? I refused to settle. I'm a good woman, not a perfect woman. There is no perfect woman but as far as I know I did everything I could do to make my partner's life easier. I did it with my first ex and with my second ex, but why couldn't they do that for me?

People say that I never let anyone do anything for me. That's because I know they won't do it right, but I did give them the chance to try. I guess I have some changes that need to be made within myself. I knew I needed to change some things and that's what led me to think maybe that's what God was waiting on me to change. I knew if I changed my ways, God could bring me that perfect person made for me. I learned in both of my past relationships that sometimes I wanna go to bed and wake up someone with someone beside me who I know loves me and appreciates me. They won't bail out on me for selfishness, stupidness or even cowardness (and if those aren't words I just made them up).

I found myself being in a lot of funks for different reasons and most of the time it was either about money situation or relationship situation I was tired of living paycheck to paycheck. I was tired of working two jobs, but I did what I had to do not only for my kids but for myself. I never let my children know when I was struggling financially which is probably why they thought we were rich. I never told them that we were because we weren't, but I definitely never let them know when I didn't have any money. They never knew that I fed them and I went to bed hungry. I never let them know that I was crying about how I was going to pay the light bill or the food bill. I felt like a child should never have those kinds of worries on their heart, so I kept that to myself and just pushed myself to do better.

Look how quickly karma comes around. My second ex found out that the girl she cheated on me with had genital warts. I'm just gonna leave that at that. I knew I didn't have it because we had been stopped having sex. I hate to say it, but I was grinning inside. I thought to myself that's what you get for fuckin' around with random bitches.

I also will admit that I almost gave into my second ex and went back with her. Why? Because of familiarity and I did not want to have to get to know someone else or have someone else get to know me all over again. I was adamant about not being like my mother bringing different people around my children having different people live with us, I did not like that, and I did not want that for me and my kids. To be clear my children only saw me with four people which was my second child's father, my first lesbian ex, the second one and eventually the current one.

Later on that year, I finally received the pay increase that I have been praying for which meant that I did not have to work a part time job. To put the cherry on top, I started having feelings for my friend who I was just being casual with. I was talking to one of my friends about my feelings. I told her how I was afraid, yet I felt bad because I was supposed to be trying to work it out with my second ex. We were supposed to be taking the time to work things out and resume our relationship after six months, but I felt like as soon as she moved out, I didn't want to work on it. I mean it was her choice to leave and I felt like she sacrificed her family for lust. I did miss her sometimes, but I didn't miss her waking me up at 2:30 in the morning getting ready for work, her allergies, being sick all the time, her whining and her selfishness. What I did miss was her paying her bills, but I know I can make it on my own. Maybe that was God's way of showing me that I could make it on my own.

Whenever I entertain the possibility of getting into a relationship, I do a comparison chart. I do a pros and cons of being with whoever it is. At the time my new young friend was possessing a lot of qualities that I was looking for. Here is the list of qualities I was looking for:

1. romance
2. passion
3. spontaneity
4. chivalry
5. trust
6. empathy
7. closeness
8. ability to give me multiple orgasms.
9. her to be giving.
10. compromise
11. mental stability
12. independent
13. job
14. car
15. money
16. educated

17. attentive
18. family oriented
19. knows how and when to take care of business.
20. good sense of humor
21. good listener advice giver
22. Not too sensitive not too insensitive
23. patient
24. understanding
25. strong willed but not stubborn
26. believes in God attends church at least occasionally.
27. effective communicator
28. appreciative

It's now 2009. I ended with two children then three then down back to two. I had a 6-year-old and a four-year-old. It was rough in the beginning getting to know my new girlfriend's daughter because she was understandably standoffish. She was a little kid and didn't know who I was. My "girlfriend" (we weren't official yet) had gotten a new job where she had to be at work for five in the morning which meant she couldn't bring her daughter to school, so I volunteered to bring her since her school was literally 2 miles from my job. My youngest daughter went to school around the corner, so the bus would bring her there and back. I made sure I was home before she left for school, and I was home when she returned.

As I stated before, my youngest daughter would lie a lot, so when she was telling the truth no one would believe her for obvious reasons. There was a time when she came home and told me that a little boy on the bus was feeling on her breasts. I asked her did she tell the bus driver and she said yes but the bus driver didn't do anything. I will admit I thought about it for a couple of days before I actually took action because I did not know if she was telling the truth or not. I ended up going to the school to make a complaint about the incident. The principle let me know that because it did not happen on school grounds, they could not do anything about it, and I would have to call the bus garage manager to let them know what happened. I did just that and the bus garage manager suspended the little boy for six weeks off of the bus. When the little boy was able to ride the bus again, he would have to sit at the back of the bus and my daughter would have to sit at the front of the bus and that was the only remedy they could offer because they both were juveniles, and they did not prosecute juveniles at that time.

Both of them were in elementary school. My daughter would have had to been in the third grade and the little boy would have been in the 4th grade. I came home and let my daughter know that she was to sit at the front of the bus from now on. To this day she tells people that she was molested, and I knew about it, and I did not do anything about it. Even though I did not believe her story, I did what I could do at the time. I did not feel bad for not believing her after finding out that it really did happen. I felt bad for her, and I felt bad that all they could do was suspend the little boy because he was a little boy. I did my part.

It was imperative that she rode the bus. I did not have the option of bringing her to school or letting her go to the daycare because I could not afford it. Her father didn't live anywhere near me so he couldn't bring her either. I did what I could do at the time with the resources that I had available to me.

After that incident came a few more years of disobedience, behavioral issues and no one even trying to help me. I reached out to my mom for her guidance and all I got was pushback basically saying that nobody did that to me when it came to the disciplinary actions. She seems to forget that what she did to me was considered child abuse. My daughter was getting in trouble so much that I didn't wanna have to spank her every time she did something, so I came up with alternative forms of discipline. I'll talk more on that later.

I reached out to my dad to see if he would be willing to be more of a father figure in her life because her dad wasn't coming around like that. At that time, I never asked her dad to be a dad. He knew he made a child. My dad can only do so much because he barely raised me, so he really didn't know what to do. When he would come get my youngest for the weekend to spend time with her, it would end up being a shopping spree for her. Therefore, no lessons were learned about her behavior.

Because I wasn't getting any help with my children, and I was too embarrassed to get help outside of the family, I reached out to my oldest daughters' grandmother. Even though me and her son were not on speaking terms, for whatever reason and he was not taking care of his child. I always thought of her as a strong woman who I could reach out to for help. I reached out to her because I learned that my oldest daughter was getting kept back a grade and I did not want that for her. At the time I did not like the school she was going to and there were no alternative schools that I knew of that I could send her to that would allow us to keep our schedule with work and school and me not having to go out of my way or pay someone to bring her back and forth to school.

I had to go back to Beaumont because I knew resources there, I was familiar with things there and I knew there were alternative schools that she could go to, and she would be placed in the correct grade. She was supposed to be in 11th grade but at the school she was in they had her as a 10th grader because of her grades. And as I stated earlier her grades were declining because she couldn't stay out of that little boy face long enough to get her work done. I even tried reaching out to the boy's mom and to let her know what was going on and she wasn't any help at all, so I ended up threatening her and telling her that if I saw him at my house again, I was going to kill him. I never saw him again after that phone call.

I thought long and hard about this before I made the decision. I talked to her teachers, I tried tutorials, but nothing could help her because she wasn't even trying to help herself. She was delusional about what grade she was in. At that time, I don't even think that she wanted the help, but I just did not want her to be kept back a grade for her sake. I asked her paternal grandmother if she could come and live with her in Beaumont so that she could go to a school and be placed in the correct grade. She was 17 years old. I knew that the district we lived in in Houston, their education system was more advanced. My daughter was fine and passing her classes, until she met this little boy who she risked it all for, but I won't go into that.

My daughter's paternal grandmother agreed to take her. She was happy to have her come and live with her. I initially asked my mom, but she said no. She says she did not want to deal with my oldest daughter's attitude and that she was mean. After my mom said no, I asked my dad if he would take her, I thought maybe she needed a father figure in her life and she did not have one because I didn't date men and I wasn't around men. My dad said no because of his work schedule and how he traveled so much he would not be there so she would essentially be home alone and that's definitely not what we wanted.

I made the hard decision of packing up her things and sending her to live with her paternal grandmother. My oldest daughter cried the whole ride. She begged me not to send her away. I tried to explain to her that it was not a punishment because it wasn't. I thought I was doing what was best for her at the time. She initially started living with her paternal grandmother and then after crying and begging my mother, she finally decided to let her come and stay.

When I dropped her off in Beaumont, I swear it felt like a whole weight had been taken off my shoulders. I felt like since she was the oldest, she was set in her ways and there was nothing I could do to redirect her. I also felt like that I could focus more on my youngest child since she was now 6 and day by day her behavior gotten worse.

My mom found out that I sent my oldest to live with her paternal grandmother she was so mad at me she stopped talking to me for a while. This was in March 2009. We had a disagreement, and I was disrespectful. I had called her back to apologize for yelling at her even though I meant what I said but I shouldn't have yelled. I asked her to listen to what I had to say. Which didn't matter to me what she thought about the way I live my life; it's my life. The decisions that I make when it comes to me, and my kids are my decisions. Just because you don't agree with them does not give you the right to undermine what I say. I don't tell you how to raise your kid and you have no right to tell me how to raise mine. I do what I think is best for my kids. If you are constantly siding with her on issues, you do not know the full story about, you are sending her a message that is okay for her not to listen to me or her grandmother. I later learned that my oldest daughter told people that I sent her to Beaumont so I could be gay. Apparently, my mother believed it. But how could she believe it because if that were true both of the kids would have been gone?

I ended up calling my dad to tell him what happened, and he gave me his support. He didn't jump on me being negative or judgmental at all. He even asked me how I felt about the situation. Nobody in my family asked me that.

I think that was one of the issues that I had with my family; no one ever asked me about my feelings. Anytime anything happened with the children they would believe whatever the children told them which was not fair to me. I knew how I could be when it came to people, but I would never purposely mistreat my children.

Over the months, my second child's behavior has gotten worse and worse. It seemed like every day or at least twice out of the week I was getting an e-mail or a phone call about her behavior. By this time, I'm in a relationship with my third girlfriend, and her child and my second child were being raised together in the same household with the same rules. I noticed that one child follows the rules and rarely ever got in trouble while the other child which was mine, stayed in trouble and always bucked the system.

I had finally found a church that was gay friendly, and it wasn't too far from home, so we decided to visit all four of us. We wouldn't go every Sunday, but we went as often as we could. The children would go to the children's church and my girlfriend, and I would attend regular service.

As far as my romantic relationship everything was okay. No relationship is perfect, we were both still teaching each other while at the same time learning ourselves and learning how to raise our children together as sisters. By 2010 I had gotten my Master's degree and Business Administration with a concentration in Human Resources Management, I had got a promotion at my job, and everything seemed fine from the outside.

After seven years of no communication or rarely any communication between my second child's father and myself, we finally started to rekindle a friendship and be co-parents to our child. I kept him informed about what was going on with our child. Once I got into a romantic relationship with my last girlfriend, I let them meet because I wanted him to know who I was letting around our child. I didn't do that previously because of course we were on the outs, and he didn't have anything to do with me.

I was trying to right my wrongs and let him into my life as a friend and the parent of our child. Whenever he had relationships, he will let me know and it did not bother me. He always told me that whoever he was with it wasn't serious, so I didn't make it a point to meet the other person because I trusted his judgment.

Whenever the school would call about our child, I would let him know. If it needed to be a parent teacher conference, I let him know and he would come if he could. Things seemed to be on the up and up as far as us co-parenting, but this did not improve our child's behavior.

Chapter NINE

HATERS SEASON

Later in 2011, my girlfriend and I felt it was time for me to buy a house. The townhome that we were living in was going up on the rent significantly. It made more sense to pay my own mortgage than to pay someone else's. It took months and months for me to find what I wanted. This was a very stressful situation to find a house and it was even more stressful when I had a child who would not behave. When we finally found the house, I put in my notice to vacate the townhome where I was living, and I let my child know that we would be moving soon, but not to tell anyone until we're sure where we were moving to. One thing I learned about my second child, she could not hold water on her chest which means she cannot keep a secret. Even though I specifically let her know that if she told anyone that we were moving she could get in trouble, and I could get in trouble. That did not stop her from running her mouth.

She went to school and told her teacher that we were moving, the teacher called me for a conference. I lied and told the teacher that no we were not moving but in fact we had already moved. I really liked the school and her teachers there, so I did not want to move her to another school just yet; but because she opened her mouth she got put out of school and I had to hurry up and find her another school to go to. I was so upset but there was nothing I could do to convince them otherwise to keep her in school at least until the end of the year.

I questioned my child and ask her why she told people that we have moved. She said that she didn't tell anyone. I will go on to ask her how they found out. I remember her vividly saying that the other kids saw us packing boxes and they must have told the school we moved. Her lying was so elaborate that if you did not know her you would believe her and therein lies our problem. We ended up moving in with my girlfriend's mom. I had to contact my daughter's dad and ask him to take her so she could go to school since he lived right across the street from the school. The school that was nearest to us at the time only went up to 3rd grade and she was in the 5th grade. He of course said yes, and then we made the arrangements to enroll her in the school nearest to him. We went back to our arrangement that we had when she was a little girl, which was he would have her a week and then I would have her a week.

It actually seemed like things were looking up. She was able to finish out the school year and was on to middle school. The school that she ended up going to was right next door from her elementary school she was attending. I was still dropping off my girlfriend's daughter to school and I was also dropping my daughter off to school. My job was near both of their schools.

With the new school came new problems. Or shall I say the same problems at a new school. Also, during the time, my child's father let me know that he met someone, and he thinks they were getting serious. I was happy for him because it was about time that he found someone that he could possibly see sharing his life with. I wasn't ready to meet her yet. I wanted to have some time pass to make sure that they will stay together because you never know with relationships.

I remember one day, my girlfriend, her daughter, and I were on the way to pick my daughter up from school. Literally as we were pulling up into the pickup line, my cell phone rang. It was the school calling. I remember thinking, "damn, what now. School hasn't even let out yet." I answered it and it was a CPS officer calling to let me know that someone reported me for child abuse and for me to come into the school's office.

I had my girlfriend park, and I went inside. I had no clue what this was about because there had been no spanking incidents. I met with the CPS officer she told me who she was. She said that someone reported me for child abuse. I asked her who and of course she told me she couldn't reveal that, but the report was that I was feeding my child dog food. I looked at her and bust out laughing, literally. I said, "Ma'am we don't even have a dog, so I wouldn't waste my money to buy dog food just to feed her as a punishment." I said, "Now if you get a report saying I'm not feeding her then believe that."

The CPS officer went on to ask me if we had food in the house and if our house was clean. I told her you're more than welcome to come see if you want to. I even said do I look like I'm going without food, I was heavier then. I wasn't even mad, I was laughing and trying to figure out who the fuck would call CPS and tell them that I was feeding my child dog food when I didn't even have a damn dog.

Of course, I went straight to my child and asked her did you have somebody called CPS on me telling them that I fed you dog food, of course she said no. Then I had to ask did you tell anybody that I fed you dog food then she said no. After probably an hour-long interrogation, she finally said that she told her dad's new girlfriend that I made her eat oatmeal and it tasted like dog food. To this day, I still don't believe that but whatever. So, I was left to assume that my child's father's new girlfriend called CPS on me believing what my child was saying. I wasn't mad at her because of course she doesn't know me but she could have been an adult and contacted me herself instead of just calling CPS, if it was her who called.

One of the punishments that I would give both children if they broke the rules or didn't behave or got in trouble or whatever was that they would go to bed without dinner one night. Or they would eat a sandwich or eat oatmeal. So, this particular night my child was made to eat oatmeal, or she could have eaten nothing, so she ate the oatmeal because she was hungry. But then, turned around and tell somebody I fed her dog food. I actually thought it was funny because this was a whole new lie that I would have to live with, and you'll see coming up.

Remember previously when I said I didn't want a spanking to be the only form of discipline that I use? I went back to my childhood when my aunt used to punish us. She used to make us stand in the corner. She used to make us hold our hands in the air and reach for Jesus. She used to put us on our knees. She used to make us write sentences. I did all of those things just so I wouldn't spank her because I knew that I could hit hard, and she bruised easily just like I do to this day. I recall one time that she was on punishment, and I had her stand on the corner, and she had pulled the paint off the wall and at the same time almost chewed a hole in her lip. I made sure to take pictures and to call her dad and let him know that she did this herself and nobody touched her. When I questioned her about why she pulled the paint off the wall she denied doing it, but she was the only one standing over there and it was clear that she did it. I also asked her why she would bite a hole in her lip and she said again that she didn't do it.

I've talked to her dad about her behavior issues, and he was helping in the beginning, but things changed later on. It was like he fell in line with everyone else and didn't believe me when I would tell him what was going on. I decided that maybe she needed to go see a child therapist. I was working part time for a child therapist, and I asked her opinion on the issues I was having, and she recommended a therapist for me to take my child to and I did.

The therapist was very nice, and she listened to both of us together and separately. I told the therapist that my child could make you think you had on a yellow shirt when you knew good and well you put on a red shirt. That's how good she was at convincing people, and it seemed like nobody would believe me because she was that good. Hell, I remember a time a teacher called the house and said that my child was so smart and talented, and she told her that she won a beauty contest when she was a baby. I told the teacher she's never been in a beauty contest. The teacher said, "Well she said she had". I had to tell the teacher that she was lying, and the teacher said, "Well she's very convincing". All I could say was, "I know." Anyway, I talked to the therapist and let her know the issues I was having and then she started seeing my child separately. After a few sessions the therapist recommended testing by a psychiatrist.

When she recommended a psychiatrist, I was like Oh my God something really is wrong with her. I remember us going to visit the psychiatrist and him performing several tests on her. I wasn't in the room. I just know we were there a long time and then he finally came out and asked to talk to me. My child waited in the lobby while the psychiatrist brought me in his office and proceeded to tell me that everything that my child was doing, she was doing it on purpose and there was no medication that was going to make her stop. He said that she was doing it because she wanted to and when she's ready to stop she will. Mind you I was not looking for medication I was looking for a diagnosis. Back then she was diagnosed with Oppositional Defiant Disorder.

The Mayo Clinic describes Oppositional Defiant Disorder (ODD) as a frequent and ongoing pattern of anger, irritability, arguing and defiance toward parents and other authority figures. ODD also includes being spiteful and seeking revenge, a behavior called vindictiveness. If you've never heard of ODD then you can read about it here: https://www.mayoclinic.org/diseases-conditions/oppositional-defiant-disorder/symptoms-causes/syc-20375831

That definition is exactly how I would describe my child at the time. And to know that there was no cure for what she was doing devastated me because I did not want her to act this way towards a stranger who would end up hurting her. It was hard for me to try to discipline my child and protect her at the same time because of her behaviors. It was definitely a case of damned if I do and damned if I don't because again, I was reaching out to my family for insight and help and they were not helping me. They did not help me because they did not believe me. Anyone who didn't see that side of my child didn't believe me.

Once we got back to the therapist with the paperwork from the psychiatrist, I asked the therapist to continue to work with her. The therapists agreed to work with her and over the weeks the therapist ended up asking to speak with me. When I went into the therapist office before my child's next appointment, I did not know what the therapist was going to say but I was open to hear it because at this point, I heard it all at least I thought.

The therapist said that my daughter told her that I said that I wish she would hurry up and die. I denied saying that. I would never say anything like that. I didn't remember saying anything like that. But much later, I did remember that I did say that. I don't remember the circumstance as if I needed one, but I do remember saying it when I was retwisting her hair. There's no excuse for what I said even if I did mean it. I don't wish death on anyone then and now. I just wanted her to stop, not die.

The therapist sat me down and looked me in my eyes and told me that I needed to do something with my child because she was trying to set me and my girlfriend up. At first, I did not understand what she meant by *set us up*, so I asked her was she meant, and she said that my child is deliberately saying things that aren't true in order to get me and my girlfriend in trouble.

All I can think of is why would she do that? What did I do to her to make her want to set me up? I'm her mother. I know my girlfriend hadn't done anything to her or at least I wasn't told that she did. I felt like I was in a *Lifetime Movie*. This could not be my life where I had to watch my back from my own blood, my own child. After that meeting with the therapist, I decided to put protective measures in place for myself and my girlfriend. We placed cameras in all of the common areas of the house. My daughter had started getting weird and I did not like it. I also reached out to a prophetess to help pray over her. Shit, I was tempted to try and find an exorcist.

The prophetess gave me holy oil to put on her every night before bed which I did and each time I did my child would just laugh. But I kept doing it anyway until I got tired because the more, I prayed it seemed like the worse she got. I started praying over her while she was sleep. I just kept praying and swear the more I prayed, the more bad things were happening.

I thought this was going to be a new beginning for everyone. We can start from scratch. In the meantime, I asked my child's father to take her for a few months until we could get secured in the house and get settled. It was the end of the school year she was in 5th grade.

He agreed, he was excited to get her. I thought it would be like it used to be when we used to alternate. Especially since we were getting along again, and we were co-parenting again. The one thing that I did not like is that he always made excuses for her behavior, but I couldn't control what he did. I could only control what I did. The biggest problem with that was, the things that I would tell him that she was doing. He never seen that side of her, so it was hard for him to believe me when I told him what she was doing. But you would have to know me to know that I wouldn't make up lies about a child. Of all the things that I could lie about, I wouldn't lie on a child.

In 2012, I finally was able to get into the house. It was a 5 bedroom, 3-and-a-half-bathroom house in a great neighborhood with great schools. At the time, each of the girls would have their own room. I chose the room based on the future; meaning I gave my girlfriend's daughter the front bedroom and gave my daughter the bedroom above our bedroom. The master bedroom was downstairs. When my child came back from being with her dad and the new school year was starting, this was going to be a clean slate.

I sat my daughter down and talked to her and let her know the rules were still the rules and I had certain expectations especially for her following the rules. The rules that I had in place were not hard. They couldn't have been hard because my girlfriend's daughter obeyed them. There was a point where I even included both children in setting the rules just to make sure that they will follow them. It all came down to my second child just did not like rules at all, but I constantly let her know that there were rules everywhere and she would have to follow them whether she liked it or not.

Anyway, even though I was progressing at work and was in a relationship, things were on shaky ground for the longest time. You never want to come home to chaos. Your home is supposed to be the one place where there is peace. There was no peace in my new home as long as my daughter was there. I remember when her dad used to come and pick her up for the weekend, I was elated. When it was time for him to bring her back, I was sad. I'm only speaking for myself but I'm pretty sure everyone else in the house felt the same way.

By this time, I could truly understand the meaning of it's always one of your children who will test your gangster, and my second child was the one. I don't want to make my child sound like she is just this awful person. All I can say is that she was awful to everyone who lived in the house. Fuck it, we were in a living hell. If you were an outsider, then she was nice to you because you didn't know her the way we knew her.

Things got so bad that I had her dad get her every weekend because that was the only way and the only time that there was peace in the house, when she wasn't there. So, he would get her every weekend and bring her back for school on Sundays. Later, I learned she would be crying and making him think she was being tortured and killed at my house. She told him that I cut her hair so that I can make her look like a boy. She told him I bought her boy clothes too. Who knows what else she was telling him, and he was believing her. This threw the co-parenting out the window.

The only thing that was happening at my house was that I was watching her. I would go through her backpack. I would go through her drawers. I would flip the mattress, pillows everything to make sure she did not have something she had no business having. Her dad didn't do that. He pretty much let her do whatever she wanted, and he believed everything she said which means I looked like the wicked bitch of the West.

It even gotten to the point where I would do locker checks at her school. I would go up to her school randomly once a week and check her locker to make sure it was clean. This is where I found out she was hiding things. She was hiding clothes that did not belong to her that I would never allow her to wear.

Apparently, she was changing into them wearing them during the day and then changing back into her clothes that she left the house in. I didn't know where she had gotten those clothes from, but I know I did not buy them. I just confiscated them and put them in the donation bag. To teach her a lesson and let her know that she was a little girl. I sent her to school with her hair combed like a little girl. Well, her daddy was mad at me for that, but I didn't care because she was a little girl. It was a mess, and I was glad for her to be going to a new school and live in our new home.

Once we got settled in our new home, I decided that she needed to go to a school in our area where my house was and during that same time her dad had moved out of town with his new girlfriend and her kid almost an hour away, so it worked out fine.

Later on, her dad notified me that he was going to marry his girlfriend and I was genuinely excited for him. There was just one thing, him and I were still legally married because our divorce never went through the first time back in 2001. I let him know this and he had the nerve to fix his lips and asked me to file for the divorce again meaning pay for it. I quickly told him no. I paid for the first time, and he didn't follow through so I damn sure wasn't gonna pay for it again. What I did do though was draw up some more divorce papers gave it to him. After I signed, he filed and paid for the divorce. It actually was done this time. The divorce had gone through 90 days later.

I was happy for him. He told me who his fiancée was and where she was from. He told me about her background. I did my own background check on her. I came back and talked to him and asked him are you sure you want to marry someone with this type of background. He swore that she was not like that anymore. I told him OK, be careful. So, that's when I decided that it was time for us to meet. After all, she was going to be my child's stepmom.

I let my child's dad know that I wanted to meet the stepmom and he told me OK, but the meeting never happened. I kept asking, "Hey when are we going to meet, I would like to meet her? The same courtesy that I gave him to meet my girlfriend and her daughter was the same that I wanted in return. I remember one night on a drop off we met at our usual spot so that we could do the exchange. I saw that he had his girlfriend in the car, so I said, *"Let me go and just meet her real quick just to say hi."* I went to the driver side because her dad was driving, and I stuck my hand in the window, and I said, "Hi, how are you" She didn't say anything back and she was on the phone, so I said well maybe she didn't hear me so I went around to the passenger side and tapped on the window so she can let it down and I stuck my hand in the window, and I said, "Hello my name is Shawnti I'm her mom." Let's just say that she was not enthused to be introduced to me.

I also met her daughter, and she was happy to meet me. I thought she was such a beautiful little girl. Later my child's dad told me that him and his fiancée had an argument because he told her that she was being rude to me. I let him know that was OK it might have been uncomfortable for her we'll just meet another time.

Some time had passed I was still having issues with my child. Things were just getting more frequent with her behavior issues and I still wasn't getting any help or insight from family or her dad. Her dad came to me and said that he was about to get married, and I said, "Great now we really need to have a sit down the four of us me my girlfriend you and your fiancé make that happen." He finally broke down and said that she didn't want to meet me and at the time I couldn't understand why because we never met. I've never said anything to her other than trying to introduce myself. It never crossed my mind that he told her old inaccurate shit about me that she was holding on to like it happened yesterday. But we'll get into that later.

I hated to be that kind of person but essentially, I said we are going to meet one way or the other and I told him that until I meet his fiancé that my child was not going to be spending any nights over at his house anymore. I never once said that he could not see his child. I made it clear that she wasn't spending the night. I made it clear that if he wanted to meet and take her out for the day and bring her back the same day that was perfectly fine, but he went back and told his fiancée something totally different. What I told him got translated into me saying that she couldn't see her daddy at all because I wanted to meet the fiancé first which was very incorrect. Of course, she would believe him because that's her man and she don't know me and can only believe what he tells her about me.

So, I wake up the next morning to find out that I'm being tagged on Facebook saying that I wouldn't let the daddy see the child and if I had a problem don't take it out on the child. I could not for the life of me wonder where that came from but then I had to take off my rose color shades and know that her dad told this woman that I said he couldn't see her at all until we met and that is not what I said. Her peanut gallery was chiming in and I'm like these people don't even know me. She doesn't even know me. But this was before I found out that he had told her about our relationship and how we broke up, which of course he only told the side that made him look like the victim. I'll let you in on what was told in a minute.

I never had anything like this happen to me before, so I was dumbfounded. I could not believe this was happening. I never bother anybody, and I don't do mean things to people, anymore. I'm here trying to get right and get help for my daughter who obviously has a mental issue and I'm being berated on the Internet by strangers. I'm thinking I'm doing the adult thing by contacting my child's father and letting him know to please talk to your fiancée. Let her know this isn't cool and take it down. I don't know if she ever took it down or not, I just blocked her. It was apparent that she didn't like me and that was fine with me, but I don't do the messy drama stuff, especially on the Internet.

The time passed and it got closer to their wedding date. He finally convinced her that we all needed to meet, so we did after they cancelled three times prior. I just wanted to meet her in person and let her know that I didn't have anything against her. I wanted her to get to know me and my girlfriend and I wanted to get to know her. I guess somewhere in my mind I thought that we could all get along and co-parent together. But at the time I didn't know that she had traumas of her own that she hadn't dealt with, which is why she was so against me being the ex.

I just wanted to meet her because she was going to be in my child's life. My child was drawn to her and liked her and that made me happy until I found out that she was calling her Mama and referring to me as Shawnti in their presence.

My child's father, his fiancé, my girlfriend, and I finally had a sit down at a restaurant. The meeting was to talk about our daughter and her behavior and what she was in for. I tried to warn her. She didn't want to talk to me, let alone listen to what I had to say at all. She didn't even want to look at me. I definitely was looking at her in the face and I meant what I said. I did not have anything against her and what me and my child's father had was in the past. I did not want him in any way but to be a father to our child. During this meeting the only thing she said to me was that my child's father can do what he wants. I didn't have anything against her. I didn't judge her by her past, but she definitely judged the fuck out of me from some hearsay.

Two days after the family meeting, my child's father had a new wife. My daughter was in the wedding and his new wife sent me pictures from the wedding. At first, I thought she was just sending them to show me that they got married. I responded with "Congratulations!" "I'm happy for y'all." Because I was. I was genuinely happy that he had found someone to marry and start a life with.

Keep in mind I'm now in a relationship and I love being a mom to two little girls. I was so hopeful that things would turn around, but they didn't. One night I was doing my clean-up slash make sure she doesn't have anything she's not supposed to have, and I came across a letter that was written. I couldn't tell if it was written by her or if it was written to her but nonetheless the things that were in that letter had my jaw on the floor. These kids were talking about having sex in an abandoned house, doing drugs and I immediately confronted my daughter about it.

I demanded her to read the letter aloud and she didn't want to read it because it had vulgar language in it. I told her it was OK because I knew she cussed I wanted her to read that letter. She refused to read the letter so much that she said she was leaving, as in she decided to run away. I let her know that if she walked out of that door she wouldn't be coming back. When I tell you she bolted out the front door in her pajamas and no shoes on and was gone. At the moment I had to laugh at it because I couldn't believe she actually left. In the meantime, I was advised to call the police because she was under age, and we weren't going to look for her. We needed to put on record that she ran away, and I did just that.

I then got a call from one of my Mason brothers telling me that he saw my daughter walking down the street. He picked her up and brought her to my aunt's house who lives maybe 10 minutes down the street. I asked him why he took her there. He should have brought her back home. He said that he didn't know what was going on and she was hysterically crying. I was low key mad at him because if I'm your sister and you're my keeper you should have called me first. But I know he was thinking as an educator and not as a Mason brother. I let it go and thanked him for letting me know where he took her. I never got a call from my aunt saying that my daughter got dropped off to her house either.

A few minutes later I get a call from her dad asking what happened. In the middle of me telling him what happened he starts screaming, blaming me for my daughter's behavior and making threats towards me. He had never spoken to me like that before. I just hung up the phone. I just couldn't believe all this was going on. He was not the same person that I knew, so that only told me that somebody was in his ear. She wanted him to hate me as much as she hated me. *She* is his wife.

The police came to the house and took my report. I gave him all the information that he asked for and I let him know that we found out where she was. He escorted us to my aunt's house. I rang the doorbell, and my aunt answered the door and her face dropped when she saw the police behind me, and she hurried up and called my daughter to come downstairs. When she was coming downstairs, she had this big old grin on her face, and I was wondering what the fuck she was happy about. She never looked up until she got to the bottom of the stairs and when she did, she saw me and the police there. Her smile quickly turned into a frown. Her dad apparently told her he was on his way to get her, and she thought it was him at the door. He never told me that she had called him. He never even tried to come and get her like he has her thinking he would.

The officers laid into her. They did kind of a *Scared Straight* episode on her. One of the officers told me to whip her ass when we got home. To this day, I appreciate the officers for that. Not that I needed their permission, but they soon saw the circumstance and so it was justifiable for her to be punished for her actions. When we got home, I didn't whip her. I just told her to go to bed. I'd had enough for the night.

I went to bed that night crying my eyes out. All my girlfriend could do was hold me and let me cry. I was crying for many reasons. But mainly, asking God why are you punishing me? How much longer do I have to endure this pain? I was tired. Mentally tired. Looking back God wasn't even halfway done yet. There was more pain to come.

Later on, I found out that she didn't want to read the letter. She denied that it was even hers and that she was holding it for someone and that it was song lyrics. I don't know why young people think that people my age (at the time I was 34 years old) don't know anything and didn't listen to the radio. Just because I didn't listen to the radio in front of them, I did listen to it. What I saw on that letter was not any song lyrics.

Things seemed to be looking up when it was time for 8th grade. She came back home from spending the summer with her dad right before school started. She started acting better. She went to a new school with new people, and I thought this was going to be a fresh start. She wasn't getting into trouble as much. She had even been assigned to be an office helper at school and she was aware that she couldn't get in trouble. She was supposed to be setting an example for the other students. This made her feel good, and this made me feel good. Her dad and I were still cordial and talking.

Then one day I get a call from one of her teachers requesting a parent teacher conference. I let her dad know and then me my girlfriend and her dad went to go talk to the teacher. The teacher said she was acting weird and essentially was boy crazy, something I already knew. Her dad of course was in denial and making excuses for her. When we got home, I talked to my daughter again about behaving and just left it at that. I knew it went in one ear and out the other.

The next day when I went to work, I began researching places that I could send my child to that was in house care for her ODD. I did all the research. I found at least five places that would accept her, but her dad had to agree to it too. I knew that he wouldn't. I wasn't trying to send her away to get rid of her, I was trying to send her somewhere so she could get the help she needed. I didn't know at the time that ODD was a new thing, but I knew that I wasn't professionally or mentally equipped to deal with it and neither was he because he was in denial about our daughter's behavior.

I got all my information together and approached my child's father on the idea of sending her to one of these group homes. He immediately said no and that he would take her. I did not want her to live with him because I knew she wasn't going to get the help she needed. She was only going to get the platform to continue doing what she was doing or even worse. I didn't want his new wife and stepdaughter to have to deal with what we had to deal with. It would not have been fair to them, but he refused to sign off on her going to a group home.

The following week I get a phone call from the office secretary at school. She let me know that my daughter had been removed from being the office helper because she was found cursing in the hall and that's not the example that the school wanted in an office helper. I completely agreed and understood, and I wasn't even mad about it. I was tired. I was exhausted. I had enough. From kindergarten to now 8th grade it was chaos. Chaos at home and chaos at school with her behavior and I was at my wits end.

I called my child's dad and asked him to come to my office so that we could talk. He came to my office the next day. He started off by apologizing to me for yelling at me during the incident when she ran away. I accepted and I asked him how he would feel about letting our child live with him. He said he was ok with it. This was a very hard decision that I had to make, but at this point it was either me going to jail and losing my job or letting her go live with him since he refused to sign for her going to a group home. Nothing was working, therapy wasn't working, nothing I was doing was working, nobody was helping, so I'd just given up.

I asked him to set up a time where we all could talk, meaning me, him and his new wife. He told me no, he could talk to her himself because she didn't want to talk to me. I asked him was she downstairs and he said yes, she was in the car. I was about to go downstairs and go get her myself so she could come up and we could talk, and he said no. He begged me not to go get her. I didn't know why at the time, but I obliged him.

I had papers drawn up regarding the details meaning I would take him off of child support and that he would have full custody of our child. I even had visitation stipulations in there because I had a feeling that once she went over there, I wasn't gonna see her. I did let him know that once she goes over there it's gonna be a minute before I will want visitation. I was disconnected at this point. I had no emotion regarding my child. I just wanted the problem to go away.

At this point we hadn't set a date when she would leave. I was actually thinking the end of the school year, but it happened much quicker than that. But then again, here's another phone call I'm getting about her behavior at school. I was sick and tired. I was done I didn't want to do this anymore.

Everything was settled. We both signed the documents that I prepared, and we both agreed to it. He left a few minutes later and texts me and said his wife was ok with it. And I thought, *"well that was quick."* I just said OK. A few hours later I get a text from his wife that told me otherwise. She was totally against his child coming to live with her and her child and her father. She knew he had a kid before they got married, just like she had a kid, but anyway I digress.

In the meantime, I was so upset and tired of her embarrassing me for no reason, so I said I'm going to embarrass her. That same day I met my daughter at the bus stop. The children apparently knew who I was and when they saw me, they said "Oh yo mama here!" I heard her telling them to call the police as she was exiting the bus.

When she got off of the bus, I took her by her ear and walked her to the house. I remember this one lady in the car who saw us she looked at me and gave her nod of approval. Not that I needed it, but it was appreciated. I took her by the ear, walked her home while telling her that I was sick and tired of her bullshit. I never really cussed at my kids, but today I let it all out. I was so frustrated and out of it. She made a motion like she was bucking up to me, so I slapped the shit out of her with an open hand. I made her go upstairs to her room and I came back outside for air. I'm sitting there in my garage blowing off steam and at the same time wondering why there was a group of kids across the street looking over here at me. And next thing I know a police car pulls up. Here we go again.

The police officer walks up greet us and asks us to go in the house so we could talk because standing outside was a distraction with all the kids. We went inside at the front door, and he asked was everything ok. I told him what happened, and he said OK and left. A few minutes later he came back ringing the doorbell apologizing and saying that he must take a look at my child because the kids across the street are telling him that she's being abused. The kids told the police officer that I lock my daughter in the room, I don't feed her, I make her stand in the corner for hours and I make her exercise.

I told him that he was free to look around the house and, in the refrigerator, to see that we have food and people are being fed here. I told him that he could go upstairs to both of my kids' rooms to see that they had doorknobs with no locks on them, so there was no way I could lock her in her room. I told him it was fine, and I called my daughter down so he could see her. He took his flashlight and looked her up and down and talked to her and asked her was she ok. She said "yes". He asked her was she hit, and she said "yes", and he shined a flashlight on her face, and he said, "Did she hit you with an open hand?" she answered "yes", he said "Ok, that's fine as long as it wasn't a fist." He asked her has she eaten. She said "yes". He asked her was she being locked in her room she said "no." He then said to me that he was going to write those children a citation for calling the police and he apologized to me once again and he left.

The next day here's another call from school about my child's behavior. At this point, I was done. I called him and told him to pick her up from school and take her. Don't even bring her to the house. I will pack her things and he can come and pick them up later. He agreed and that was that.

This is when the harassment started by his wife. If I wasn't getting harassed and threatening texts, I was getting phone calls to my job. I was getting threats from different numbers. It was just crazy. This was the kind of shit you read about, and I had never experienced anything or anyone like this before. I damn sure wasn't about to stoop to her level. So, I let her act out on her own.

The first message was accidentally sent to me. She was talking about me but was meant to send it to someone else. It read along the lines of she was mad about her husband making big decisions without her and how she shut that shit down. She realized she accidentally sent me the text and sent another text saying, "oh sorry honey wrong text". Me and my child's father were still talking so I sent him a screenshot of what she sent me and apparently, he confronted her about it. She then comes with another text which begins the threats.

She goes on to say how she screenshot shared on Facebook how I gave up my first child and I gave up my second one and I got knocked up at 14 and for me to run a background check on her and if I say something else to my child's father about it then she was gonna tell all my business. I never responded to her. I never addressed her. From what I was told by her husband she was OK with it but apparently, she wasn't.

I can understand her being upset, but she was mad at the wrong person. As I stated earlier, I asked him to include her, and he begged me not to. Hell, I didn't want her over there to begin with. I wanted her in a group home. She had become so aggressive and demanding I guess she was used to having that attitude and getting away with it with other people, but that wasn't working on me. All of the times that I wanted to meet with her to talk about my daughter, she refused. Now that my daughter was going to live with them, she wanted to talk. I did not want to talk to her then, and I never did.

She was so pissed that I was not responding to her that she began calling my job. Things got so bad that I had to notify my job security office and they made me go and file a police report for my safety. She was calling the emergency line screaming at the people answering the phone, thinking it was me. Don't get it twisted, I ain't no snitch and I wasn't scared of her. I didn't want to lose my job. I even let my child's father know what was happening and he told me to do what I needed to do. They had her picture posted at the security door to not let her on the premises.

I ended up having to block her from my phone because she had my number. She was sending me messages with the impression that I was trying to run her house. I never said anything of the sort. What I did say is that I didn't need her permission for my child to live with her father, which I didn't. She even tried the low blow and say that I won't know what marriage is about and I won't ever know because at the time gay marriage wasn't legal. She was trying to say everything to get me to bite and I never did.

This harassment went on for almost two years before it finally stopped. I just kept ignoring her texts and thought to myself that eventually she will get tired. It took a minute, but I guess she did get tired. I had to stop and think to myself why is she lashing out like this? Why does she keep contacting me even though I'm not responding? She was even texting me through her friend's numbers and Google numbers.

Remember when I said earlier that my child's father told her things about me when we were together, that made him look like the doting father and I was just the neighborhood thot. She made it her business to bring up all the past inaccurate stories and threatened to put it on Facebook and send it to my job. I thought it was funny because the things she was saying wasn't even true. I don't know if she ever posted it or not and I don't care because I know they weren't true, so I wasn't even bothered.

When she saw that she wasn't getting her way she thanked me for ruining her marriage, which I did not. She agreed to let my child live with her father as if she had a choice. Her child was there, why couldn't his be? But that's none of my business and I stayed out of it.

She went from being against my daughter living there to now threatening that she's gonna tell everybody that I gave up my child, I'm trifling, and I had sex with my child's father's friend (which was my first girlfriend by the way). I knew her first. She never was his friend until after me and her broke up. Then she started calling my daughter her new daughter and they were going to sit around and talk about me and I'm a no-good dirty ass pussy eating hoe. She was gonna tell everyone at my job what kind of person I was and how dumb I was for letting my child come and live there with all that animosity and that's why my child can't stand me. And all I know how to do is fuck women in a hotel room. It was crazy! I couldn't do nothing but laugh, because I knew none of that shit was true. But she believed that deep down in her heart that it was. She even said that she was gonna teach my daughter and won't have her reading the Bible all day. Which means my daughter lied and told them that I had her reading the Bible all day, and that wasn't true. (And if it was, so what? It was the Bible!) And then telling me that she can run back everything that go on in my house. When I tell you me and my girlfriend sat back and laughed at all of this because she was really believing it. All I thought was, she's gonna see soon enough for herself and I guarantee you she did, and it didn't take long.

She even went as far as calling my mom and dad as if they were gonna whip my ass and make me take my child back. I didn't understand how she went from telling the world that I wouldn't let him see his child to now being mad because his child living with them. Apparently, she didn't put two and two together.

I did not understand how a grown woman who kind of went through the same thing with her ex-husband could do this to me. But like I said, hurt people hurt people. She was hurt and, in the end, she wanted to make sure I was hurt. I never responded to any of her messages, calls or threats. Not one time. What I did instead was started praying for her. Every night I prayed for her healing because she was obviously hurt. I prayed to God for her to leave me alone. I am not the enemy. If anything, I wanted us to be a cordial extended family where we could talk and help our daughter. At least she quit contacting me for now.

I held up my end of the agreement that my child's father and I made. I submitted for child support to be closed against him. We had a court date and which we both had to show up and we did. We stood in front of the judge holding hands convincing them that we were back together, and child support didn't need to be filed on him anymore. The case was dropped. Against everyone's better judgment who I spoke about this with I had even agreed to pay him child support for the four years that she was supposed to be living with him. Even though he wasn't paying me shit, I was just trying to do the right thing because I know she needed things and I know that they did not prepare to have an extra child in the house.

The first day that she moved in was on a Friday. She called me, and we were talking. When her stepmom found out that she was on the phone with me she made her get off the phone and told her that she didn't want her talking to me on the phone that she purchased. I thought that was the most childish thing a person could do but again I wasn't going to argue, and I did not. I would just talk to her on her dad's phone.

When she had school functions, he let me know and I will go to some of them, not all of them. I didn't want any confrontation. I just wanted to show up for my child even though we were on the outs, I was still her mother. It got to a point where I quit showing up for her events because of the tension and animosity that I had towards her and her father. My mom and dad would go in my place, and I was fine with that. I had no shame, fear, doubt or remorse for the decisions I have made regarding the relationship with my youngest daughter. I just couldn't wait to start hearing the stories about what she was doing over there with them.

Her stay with her father didn't last long because the real her came out and they began to see everything that I was saying. She couldn't come back to my house. I made that clear, so he sends her to his mom's house. That's when I stopped paying him child support. And that's all the energy I'm putting into that part of my story.

My relationship, on the other hand, was on shaky ground. You never really know a person until you move in with them. My girlfriend moved in along with her daughter and things were great until they weren't. Sometimes I felt like she prioritized her daughter and made concessions for her daughter, and you can tell that there was a difference of treatment. Then there were issues happening between the two of us. When we were getting to know each other, I let her know that I did not like to argue. I grew up in a house where there was arguing and when someone tries to argue with me, I shut down.

I also don't know that when someone yells at me, I stop listening. I didn't like people yelling at me or pointing their finger at me. Both of those were triggers for me from childhood. The yelling was a trigger because my momma used to yell all the time either at us kids or at whoever she was dating at the time. The finger pointing was a trigger for me because in high school a substitute teacher pointed her finger in my face, and I told her if she didn't remove it, I was gonna bite her finger off. The teacher got mad because another teacher heard what I said and laughed so she sent me to the principal's office. I got ISS which is what we called short for in school suspension.

No matter how much I used to tell her that I did not like those things especially the yelling. She was a yeller. She gave an excuse that she couldn't help it because of where she was from that's how they talk. She called it passion not yelling. I called it yelling and not passion. So along with the issues I was having with my second child and now her dad and fiancée I'm now having issues in my personal relationship. Thank God I was not having any issues at work.

At this point how things were going, I was prepared to let her go. However, I wanted to try one last time to have a successful relationship, so I convinced myself that we can work through it. I had it in my mind that she just needed to be loved a certain way and I was going to do my best despite everything I was going through. I wanted to give her what she needed even though I was going without. Little did I know, at the time, that she hadn't received any love. I believe I was her first and I'm not talking about sexual I'm talking about genuine love like you would get from a parent or family member. This is called unconditional love.

There was so much going on during this time that I almost forgot to mention that I befriended someone who later became my best friend. Around the time that I met my girlfriend someone messaged me asking who I was. Me with an attitude message back saying you messaged me first so who is this? She told me who she was and then I remembered oh I know who you are.

I met this person back when I was with my second ex-girlfriend. We were all acquainted at a party. It never went any further than hello and by at the time, I didn't even know her name, but I heard negative things about her. Fast forward to 2008, we began frequently messaging each other. It was very casual and I wasn't thinking anything of it going further than that. It was just having someone to communicate with while at work when it was slow. We would chat through messenger during the day and that's it. We later started emailing and messaging and then it turned into texting and talking.

We'd grown pretty close, and it wasn't anything other than a friendship. She did let me know that she was interested in being more than friends, but I told her that I could not date anyone who dated someone that we hung out in the same circle with. That was just one of my rules. I didn't care if I knew the person or not.

If we hung out in the same group and we both had someone back at the time and we're not with them anymore there's no way me and that person are gonna get together. I felt like that would have been breaking a code or something and I was adamant about keeping a clean reputation. She was older than me and very smart which was pleasant. It took almost two years (2014) for us to finally start having lunch together during our lunch breaks. We worked on the same side of town, so maybe once a week we would pick a day and we would meet at different restaurants by us just to get away from our offices. I enjoyed her company, and she enjoyed mine. She was in a relationship with someone and so was I.

When I met my girlfriend, she knew I didn't have any friends that lived in the city. She knew about my best friend who lived in another city, but I didn't have anyone here that I hung out with. So, when I mention my new friend to her, she wasn't exactly thrilled. Assured her that it was nothing but a friendship it was straight platonic because that's what it was. Over the years we'd gotten so close that we started talking about our relationships to each other.

She was having trouble in hers and I was having trouble in mine along with the issues with my second child. I didn't have anyone to talk to, so I talked to her. Just like everyone else she didn't agree with the decision that I made to send my daughter to live with her father. However, she actually helped me a lot by sending me devotions and speaking the Bible to me and she even got me going back to church. She comes from a very religious background and a close-knit family. I found myself wanting the exact same thing, but I knew I did not have it in my own family.

We started inviting each other out to functions along with our significant others and we were having a great time. Only one thing, her girlfriend didn't like me, and my girlfriend didn't like her. My girlfriend didn't like her because she said that my friend had more than friendly feelings for me. I couldn't see it, but she kept saying it. I don't know why her girlfriend didn't like me, but I didn't care. I will admit I didn't like her because of what my friend would say about her.

Time passes and my friend and I are still just friends however, I do admit that I was so jealous of her family relationship. By this time both of my grandparents were gone, and we all know that once the grandparents died, the family falls apart, and mine did just that. My family wasn't close. We didn't hang out anymore. Cousins stopped talking to each other and it was crazy. It was crazy how the same people that you grew up with who should have been your best friends now act like they don't even know who you are. They don't come around and when they do it's fake as fuck. I digress.

I loved how her family was together. Yes, they were not perfect, but they were more than what I had in my life. This made me sad. I'm not saying I wanted her family; I'm saying that I wanted a family like hers or I wanted my family to be a family. I always had in my mind that my family would be like the Huxtables. That was a bubble that burst really quick. I can recall crying to my girlfriend about how I wanted a family and how I wanted my family to be, and she told me to get that dream out of my head because my family is not like that, and they probably never will be. She was right.

The issues that I was having in my relationship with my girlfriend became more drastic. The arguments were happening more, and I just didn't understand it because again I wasn't used to arguing with anyone I was with. With my first girlfriend, the only argument that we had was the one after I found out she was cheating on me. My second girlfriend, we didn't argue until I found out she was cheating on me. I had to think to myself, where we are going, because my third girlfriend was cheating on me too? I didn't know what to think other than it was lowering my self-esteem and had me doubting myself. I was feeling low and like I did not deserve to be in a healthy loving relationship. I had already lost my oldest daughter. I lost my second daughter, and my mom and I were not on speaking terms. Now, me and my third girlfriend were not getting along.

The only good things that were happening in my life at the time was my job where I'd gotten a promotion again. Thank you God and my best friend who was there for me emotionally. Everything else had gone to shit.

My girlfriend was adamant about me not talking to anyone about our business. But I couldn't help it because I wanted an outside opinion on what I was doing wrong. I just needed to know what it was about me that no one understood me or liked me. Here I am thinking I'm just this nice sweet calm person who doesn't like conflict. Why couldn't anyone else see that?

During this time of going through it with my girlfriend and being harassed by my child's father's wife, I just wanted to run away from everything and everyone. But then there was a period of calm. In my mind, I know it was the calm before the storm because based on my past experiences anytime it got too quiet something big was about to happen and usually it was bad.

The calm lasted awhile longer than usual so I took it as an Amen thank you Jesus. I wasn't being harassed anymore by my child's father's new wife. My girlfriend and I were getting along. I'm still friends with my best friend. Work was going well. It was a dream come true.

November of 2015 my girlfriend and I decided to take the big plunge. We decided to get married. This was shocking to both of us as we both swore that we would never get married again. Like I said, I never had any intentions on getting married and she did not either but we both did against our better judgment. But this time was different, and we were determined to make it work.

We went to the courthouse got our marriage license and we decided on a date to get married which ended up being November 17, 2015. This is the day I became Mrs. Shawnti Refuge. I was so happy this time around. I was marrying the love of my life, and nobody was making me do it. When we exchanged vows, I was so eager to say I do that I kept interrupting the judge. I didn't hesitate to say I do. I didn't hesitate to solidify our nuptials with a kiss. I knew this was meant to be.

After our ceremony she went to get the truck and I waited for her at the front of the courthouse, and I was crying my eyes out. I was crying because I was happy. I was crying because this is what I wanted. I was crying because I finally have found someone who loved me and actually wanted to build a life with me. I was crying because I knew that this was going to be forever. There were no regrets.

And if that was so, why didn't I tell my best friend about it? No one was at the ceremony but me my wife Angela and the judge and bailiff. Why didn't I invite my best friend to be my maid of honor? I decided to tell her over one of our lunch meetings that we would have. Well not exactly. She saw the ring on my finger and slapped my hand and asked me what that was. I told her I got married and she was upset. Understandably because I didn't tell her about it, and I didn't invite her, and we were supposed to be best friends. She even asked why I didn't invite her.

I didn't tell her because I knew she would object, especially after the things I was saying about how our relationship was going. I didn't invite her because I did not feel like she was going to be really happy for me getting married to Angela. Again, based on what I was telling her. However, we did get married during a time when things were going well, and they were going well for a few months after we got married.

Shortly after our wedding we went to Cozumel for our honeymoon for a week and it was great. When we got back home it was business as usual things were still quiet and then of course the honeymoon was over quickly.

We were back to having silly arguments and I just didn't know what to do. Like I said I was adamant about keeping my marriage I was not going to have two failed marriages I was not going to be married two or three times like my mother. I also was having emotions about what happened with my child and her father and his wife, so I decided to go ahead and find a therapist.

I looked for a therapist who was black and a woman. I finally found one who was kind of an older lady, and she was close to my job so I could easily go there and come back during the day. The first session was fine considering that was my first time going to therapy. We talked about things and what was going on with me and she said we were going to work on a plan so that I could overcome the issues I was having. I made some confessions to her that I never made to anyone in my life at that time.

I let my best friend know that I was going to a therapist. She said she was considering going to one too so at the time I thought this therapist was a good one, so I recommended her to go to her. I gave her my therapist's information and never asked her again about it.

I was in this for the long haul, and this was just the beginning. Months were going by, and we still weren't getting along. I found myself confiding in my best friend about my relationship. We would talk on the way to work, during the day, and on my way home from work. My wife would find it strange that we only talked during the day. I didn't talk to anyone while I was at home for a few reasons. In this case being that I would be talking about her, I didn't want her to hear me talking about her to someone else. It's not that I was talking bad about her again I was just trying to figure us out. It was very complicated, and I couldn't talk to my wife about my wife. She would shoot down anything I would say.

After a few months and talking to my mom about how she was on antidepressants, I ended up going to my primary care physician and asking for antidepressants. I thought that these would help me to be a better person because I clearly had no idea what was going on in my life or how to fix it at the time. My doctor asked me why I was asking for antidepressants, and I told her what was going on in my life. She giggled and told me that I was going through perimenopause.

I never heard of this before, so I was like perimeno what? All I heard was menopause and I'm like I'm too young to be going through menopause. I don't even think I was 40 yet. Perimenopause means "around menopause" and refers to the time during which your body makes the natural transition to menopause, marking the end of the reproductive years. Perimenopause is also called the menopausal transition. https://www.mayoclinic.org/diseases-conditions/perimenopause/symptoms-causes/syc-20354666 She gave me the antidepressants and I went on my way.

My best friend was having issues within her relationship and the tables were turned now that she was confiding in me about her feelings and the things that were going on in her relationship. Her family planned a family vacation and at the last minute her girlfriend was uninvited. There was an extra seat, and it was offered to me and without thinking I took it. At the time the thought behind it was I needed to get away because I really felt like my marriage was ending as quickly as it began. We hadn't even been married a year and it was chaotic.

I was taking the antidepressants, but I didn't feel like they were working. And was thinking that a vacation away it was just what the doctor ordered especially since we had not had any time apart since 2008 and this was 2016. In July of 2016, I went on vacation with my best friend and her family. We went overseas to a place that I had never been before, and my mind was blown.

This was the most beautiful, calm, peaceful place that I had ever been to. It was hot as fuck though, but the water was just right. The atmosphere was just right. The company was just right. It was 15 of us all together on the trip. I was the only person who was not family, but I fit right in, and we had a wonderful time. I think the best part of it was that it was a family trip. I'd never been on a family trip before where it was mom dad sisters' nieces and cousins. We were doing everything that I dreamed of for my family. We ate together, we saw the sights together, we prayed together, and we even had church. We were in a private villa with a maid and Butler service. The maid kept us full and kept our clothes and spaces clean. The butler kept us drunk and high. I had never gotten high on the roof of a home under the stars. I had never been waited on hand and foot. There wasn't anyone complaining. I had absolutely no responsibilities and no worries. I was living my dream life even if it was only for a week.

One night during the vacation my best friend's mom sat me down and talked to me. I don't know what my best friend had told her mom about my relationship but gathering from what she was telling me it wasn't good things. Her mom told me that I deserve better I should not be in a situation where I'm not happy. I am a strong, smart and beautiful woman and I'm settling. So, saying without saying she told me to leave my wife. Most of the things she was saying I did agree with but at the same time she didn't know Angela, just like my best friend didn't know Angela. They can only go by what my best friend was saying about Angela based on what I was saying about Angela. This made me realize that I wasn't saying very good things about her. At the time there wasn't anything good to say because we were going through the ringer. It still wasn't an excuse to talk bad about my wife to someone else and I am regretful for that.

Right before I left for the trip, we got into a huge argument, and I had planned on telling her that we were over when I got back from my vacation. She took her a vacation and took her daughter and her mom back home to where she was from for a week. I think she needed the time away just as much as I needed the time away.

When I got to where I was, I rarely contacted her. I even had taken my wedding ring off and didn't wear it during the trip. I did not take my antidepressants because I didn't need them because nothing was wrong. Everything was right; too right. Everything that my best friend and I did, we did it as if we were a couple. We were holding hands, taking pictures, expressing PDA and everything you would do with someone who you were in a relationship with. I know it wasn't real, alright or right, but I was enjoying the moment for what it was, just a moment.

On the 5th night of our vacation my best friend and I went to the beach, and we sat on the beach chairs next to each other and we were smoking and talking. My best friend broke down and poured her heart out about her relationship and how she was hurt, and I did the same thing. We were both smoking and crying and smoking and crying. Finally, we decided to go back to the house and clean up.

We shared a room that had two queen size beds in it. Every night she slept in her bed, and I slept in my bed and tonight wouldn't be any different. We decided to take a shower together. The shower was big enough to where she had her side, and I had my side. We were both upset and basically grieving our relationships. How could we both be in paradise and be grieving? This was not the place to do it. Before I knew it, I walked over to her side of the shower and started kissing her and it didn't feel wrong. It felt right. We got out the shower dried off and she asked me what are we doing? I told her I didn't know but I didn't want to stop. I cheated on my wife. You can use your imagination from there.

After my infidelity I had no remorse until Angela called me. When I saw her name come up on the caller ID, I was like oh shit. I answered the phone and tried to sound as normal as I could, but she knew something was wrong. I was trying to take the attention off of me and ask her how her vacation was going. She was having a great time. So going back home to visit was what she needed.

The day after I cheated on my wife, I told my best friend that we needed to talk about what happened the night before, so we walked down to the beach, and we talked. We agreed that what happened was not going to happen again because it was wrong and that we would keep it to ourselves because we did not want to hurt anyone. Keep in mind, she had a girlfriend, and I had a wife. We had sex again that night.

On the 7th day it was time to leave and come back to the states. I was so not ready to come home because I did not want to face my reality. We got back to the states and Angela was to pick me up from my best friend's house. I cried because I did not wanna go home. I wanted to go back where we were and live in this fantasy land. My best friend held me while I cried as we were waiting for Angela to come pick me up.

Angela pulled up and said she was there. It took forever to come out of that house. It was like walking the green mile. We came out and I got in the passenger seat and my best friend put my luggage in the back. Angela and my best friend didn't say much to each other. Angela could sense something was wrong, but she didn't say anything. We made very small talk going back to the house.

Now we're back into our real lives and we were supposed to keep what we did back in paradise. Leave it to me to bring it back to the states. The day after we returned, we had plans to go to a concert and then dinner after. It wasn't supposed to be a date, but I turned it into one. At the concert, again we were holding hands as we were walking to our seats. Guilt instantly set in when I ran into someone who recognized me and who knew at least that Angela was my girlfriend. She saw me here holding someone else's hand. This was the first time I felt guilty about what I did and what I was doing.

It was two weeks after I came back from my vacation that I had to tell her what I had done. It was hard but it was necessary because she didn't deserve it no matter what problems we were having. I ended up telling her what happened and how it happened and of course the Sagittarius in her wanted to know every detail blow by blow, and I gave it to her.

She had already sensed that I had done something. She was just waiting for me to tell her. She was hurt and that was very understandable. She felt betrayed which she was because I was trying to get my best friend and my wife to be friends. Angela felt all along that my best friend had romantic feelings for me and I kept denying it because I literally did not see it. She gave me an ultimatum and told me to choose. She gave me two weeks to make a decision that would affect three people.

I was back in therapy telling my therapist what happened. She didn't offer me any help she was just listening. I had weekly appointments with her, but it didn't dawn on me at the time that I wasn't leaving better than how I came. I had gotten to feel like I was just telling her my business and she was just taking it all in.

During that time, I was still talking to my best friend, and she revealed that she wanted to be with me. This made things even more difficult because before then she never made any reference or suggestion that she liked me in that way. Remember when I said before they when I had to make a decision, I weighed the pros and cons. I did it again when I had to choose between my wife and my best friend who wanted to be my girlfriend.

While I'm making this list my best friend had already decided my life for me, she told me that I was going to sell my house, get rid of my dog and move on her side of town. Why was I in shock at this? I didn't want to sell my house. This was my dream home. I didn't want to move and at the time I didn't want to get rid of my dog. This really made me think about what the fuck am I getting myself into?

I told another friend what happened, and she helped me in determining what I wanted to do with my life. I took a piece of paper drew a line down the middle wrote Angela's name on one side and my best friend's name on the other side. Yes, I'm still calling her my best friend because she was my best friend. I listed the qualities of Angela and the qualities of my best friend. I listed what I wanted out of a relationship and put whoever 's name fit. On paper my best friend won. In my heart my wife won.

I chose to stay with my wife and work through it because we have been together since 2008 and it was now 2016. She was there through all the bullshit I was going through with my second daughter. I was there for her through the things she was going through. (I'm not mentioning it because this book is about my story and nobody else's). We were a team. She is the Ying to my Yang and I was not going to give up a bond like that. I let my wife know that I chose her, and I continue to choose her every day; even on the bad days.

Now that I've chosen my wife, I had to prove myself to her and gain her trust back. This was the beginning of my transparency. I did not want to have any secrets. I did not even want her to think that I was doing anything that I shouldn't be doing. After all we were coming up on our one-year wedding anniversary. I decided to recommit myself to her.

In the meantime, I had to tell my best friend that I did not choose her as my lover. She did not take it well. Actually, she didn't take it the way I thought she would take it. I saw the real her when she did not get what she wanted, which was me. I wanted to keep her as a friend, but I knew that would not be possible if I wanted to work on my marriage, so I had to end our friendship.

When I tell you I mourned this friendship. I mourned. This was the first person that came into my life, and I actually trusted with my secrets. I trusted her with everything and it's my fault that I gave her that much trust. It's my fault that I had an affair during a weak moment. If I could do it all again, I would rather have the friendship. Sometimes I miss her so much that I wanna call her to see how she's doing but I don't because I know if my wife found out that she would be devastated.

This person was allowed into our life and from my wife's point of view she betrayed that trust. I let my wife know that I was the initiator. Yes, my best friend could have said no but she was at a weak moment as well. We were both weak, we were both hurting. We wanted to feel good even if it was for a temporary moment. Leave it to me to get carried away and try to bring it back to the states. Needless to say, I did not have any boundaries. I did not trust myself. I was impulsive. And those three things are a dangerous combination.

HEALING + LIVING

I was back to not having anyone to confide in when I was having issues, so I held it in and kept it to myself. Yes, I had acquaintances and a few friends, but you can't tell all of your friends all of your business. Each friend serves a different purpose in my life and this one now my ex best friend was the person who I divulged a lot of information to about my relationship with Angela.

Needless to say, July 2016 was the absolute worst month ever, not only for my wife but for me as well. Not many people would stick by me after I confessed to having an affair and then turn around and have to hear me crying about losing my best friend, but she did. During the next few months and even years I did everything I could to make her know that I was dead ass serious about keeping her as my wife. We were coming up on our one-year anniversary. Prior to this, we agreed that I would take the odd number years and she would take the even number years to come up with how we would celebrate.

I thought the perfect idea would be to renew our vows. I had a whole weekend planned for our one-year anniversary. I hired a wedding officiant, and we had a small ceremony and our suite that I booked for the weekend. Angela had no clue what I was doing. I just laid her clothes out at home and told her to show up at this time as she did. She says she trusted me, and she wanted to be with me and that was all I needed to hear. I wrote my vows to her, and I tried my damnedest to memorize them but I ended up reading my vows to her.

Angela you are my everything.

Today I am renewing my commitment to you and our marriage.

You are strong where I am weak you are focused when I am dazed.

You protect me and make me feel safe.

You make me laugh you make me think and you make me waffles.

You make me feel things I haven't felt in a long time.

each day with you I feel my heart opening up more and more and I appreciate every moment.

I promise to love you as you are respect you and show your loyalty. Grow with you support you listen to you and trust you and be patient with you.

together we will fulfill our dreams I will be your partner in all adventures we will take over our lifetime whether good or not so good for all eternity I love you with all my heart.

OK, don't be using my shit at y'all wedding, this is copy written.

As part of Angela and me working on our marriage, I asked her if we could go to couples counseling. She immediately turned that down. She felt like we didn't need counseling, but I felt like we did. I continued going to therapy until the last time I went. Something just didn't sit right. Usually, I would go out of the front door, the same way I came in. This time she had me leave out the side door, I asked her why, she told me because the lobby was full and to protect my privacy it would be better to go out the side. My dumb ass believed her.

She wanted me to go out of the side because my ex-best friend was also seeing my therapist which I did not know at the time. So here the therapist is getting two sides of the affair. I was so pissed when I found out. I ended up asking my now ex-best friend was she seeing the same therapist that I was seeing, and she confessed that she was. I went back to her one more time just a good clarification and that I was not tripping. She confirmed it. I immediately fired her.

I just could not believe what I was going through. I know that what she did was wrong, it had to be wrong right? I reported her to everybody I could report her to. I made bad reviews about her everywhere I could make them. Then I got a bill from her requesting a payment that she wasn't owed. In fact, she owed me money. I let her know that if she didn't give me my money, I was gonna make her life miserable. I had it planned in my head that I was going to make flyers with her picture on it and post them everywhere I could and in her neighborhood saying what a bad therapist she was. It wasn't about the money; it was about the conflict of interest and the unprofessionalism. How are you going to treat me and the person I had an affair with? I know that they were talking about me at my ex-best friend session because the therapist came back and told me to not leave my wife for my ex-best friend because she was crazy.

I eventually got my money back because I was bugging the shit out of her and then looked for another therapist. I found another therapist. She was also black, but she was a little younger, not too young because I didn't want to feel like I was talking to a little girl. I made an appointment. I talked to this therapist for the initial consultation. I never heard from her again for the next appointment. At first, I thought she forgot about me because at the time her business was in the process of moving to another office location. I gave her a few weeks, then I contacted her again to set an appointment. After so many tries, I came to the conclusion that she ghosted me.

So, any therapist that's reading this book, if you feel like you and your potential client would not work well together, please let them know and not ghost them. As a professional you could at least let the person know that you don't feel that you are a right fit for them and try to refer them to someone else. Ghosting a person that is coming to you for help is not good for that person's mental health. I developed abandonment issues because of this.

Because this happened it made me feel like I wasn't worth it. Then I started thinking back to my past relationships and thinking they always leave me. My first girlfriend left me. My second girlfriend left me. I had it in my mind that they always leave me, and it was a matter of time before my wife would leave me too.

As time passed by, we're still having our ups and downs in our marriage. I was ready to give up because it seemed like nothing I did made my wife happy. She kept telling me that she wanted to be my wife and I kept telling her I don't know how to be a wife. I never saw anybody be a wife except for my grandmother and from what she told me, my grandfather cheated on her. Adding not seeing my mom's first marriage because I was too young. The second one I saw she was getting her ass beat and I wasn't gonna let no nigga hit on me. So, was this what I had to look forward to and being a wife? If so, I did not want it.

I knew I was sad, but I didn't know what to do about it other than pray and I was praying. I was praying, pretending, avoiding, and denying until one Sunday in 2018. I woke up for the day and immediately I was not feeling well emotionally. It felt like I had a dark cloud hanging over my head, literally. I went on with my day feeling sad but still pushing through thinking that this funk would pass.

I was crying and crying and crying and then it turned into me being mad and upset. I was lashing out and talking crazy to people and I knew this was not me. After about a month of me acting this way Angela finally told me that I needed to go see someone because she did not know how much longer she would be able to take this.

I didn't want to lose my marriage because I was acting weird, so I decided to go to my private doctor and let her know what was happening. I told her about my mood swings and the uncontrollable crying. She said that I might be a little depressed and she gave me a low dose of antidepressants. Keep in mind I'd already been down this road, and they did not work but I was not opposed to trying it again and taking it for a longer amount of time. I took the antidepressants for six weeks and I went back to her at her direction to let her know how it worked for me.

Let me fill you in on exactly how I was acting. I was having emotional outbursts such as yelling and screaming at people for no reason. The littlest thing ticked me off. I was being mean as fuck to my wife. Hell, I was being mean to everybody. Hours of avoiding people staying in the house didn't wanna talk to anybody. If I was talking to them, it wasn't pretty. It got really bad when I was going off on someone, I could literally picture another version of myself sitting on a sofa behind me and just watching me go off on whoever I was going off on. It was weird and I didn't like it. The person who was sitting on the couch was just watching me act crazy and wasn't trying to stop me they were just looking at me and shaking their head. But it was me who was looking at me do this.

Then later I could feel that my verbal outbursts were going to turn physical because I was picturing myself harming people. I never once had the urge to harm myself. It was just other people I wanted to harm. One person in particular I pictured myself knocking on their door waiting for them to answer and when they did, I would be standing there in a black hoodie what a gun facing them and capping off. This is what scared me. I'm a lover not a fighter, or a killer.

When I went to my next appointment, I told her this shit ain't working. She chuckled and said maybe you need a stronger dose. I'll up the dose and you come back to me in 6 more weeks and let me know how you feel. She been my doctor for a very long time, so I wasn't going to go against what she was saying because I trusted her. I took the higher dose of antidepressants for six weeks and report it back to her letting her know again this shit ain't working.

She looked at me and said, "Baby I'm not saying anything's wrong with you, but I need you to go see a psychiatrist". All I'm thinking is , "Psychiatrists? Black people don't go see psychiatrists. That's white people shit." I pictured myself laying on some white lady's couch telling her about all my issues and she just writing and looking at me, judging me and handing me more drugs. That's exactly what happened minus the judging part.

I found a psychiatrist and I let her know what was going on as she gave me a higher dose of antidepressants than what my original doctor gave me. She told me to take them for 30 days and then come back and let her know how they were working. I took them faithfully every day for 30 days. Within the first few days I started feeling better meaning I wasn't crying or having outbursts. I took the meds for the 30 days, and the day after I was supposed to come back to see her and get more meds. That day, the meds had stopped working and I was back crying. This is when I decided that I didn't want to spend the rest of my life on meds to control my emotions.

The psychiatrist advised me to get a therapist. As much as I didn't want to see a psychiatrist, I really didn't want to see it therapist, but I did. I found a therapist that was near my job that I could go to on my lunch break. She was black she wasn't too old, and she wasn't too young. I went to her letting her know what my issues were and how I found her.

We began talking about my childhood. I admit I was very standoffish with her because she was a stranger, and I was always told don't talk to strangers about my business. At this point I had no choice because I needed help. After weeks of therapy, I finally let her into my life so that she could see what it was like and where I came from.

She had me start off with journaling. I was against it because again I thought journaling was for white people. I had in my head that black people didn't discuss their problems they just worked through it. They damn sure didn't write about it because somebody would find it, read it and go tell somebody else about it. For example, back in middle school my friend and I were writing notes to each other and what keep them and a box. My friend's mom found the box and opened a letter that I wrote which was talking about me having sex with one of my boyfriends. Her mom was a nurse and called me out immediately asking me was I fucking. I was scared of her mom so I said no. I was even more scared that she would tell my Mama, so I really kept saying no and she kept asking me. Even though she said I wasn't going to get in trouble, but I needed to get protection if I was, I still said no, I wasn't fucking. My lie came out because I was pregnant shortly after. This is when I was 14.

Anyway, my therapist assured me that journaling would be a way to help me to revisit my past and also face things that I had in the past so that I can heal from them. Initially I began journaling, and I did not like it because it was making me mad to have to revisit all of those bad times that I had. At my next appointment, I let her know I don't like this, and she showed me another way to journal which was guided journaling. Guided journaling is when you are answering a specific set of questions and writing the answers in a notebook. I was digging the guided journaling, so I began doing that every day. After about a week I started feeling better and I couldn't believe it.

In therapy, I was able to talk about being abused as a child. I was able to talk about my relationship with my mother. I was able to talk about middle school and how I didn't have any friends and I thought no one liked me. I was able to talk about being a teen mom and its effect on me. I had no clue back then, but me being 14 and a teen   om was a form of trauma. I was able to talk about the things that I did to my second child's father. I talked about my relationship with my second daughter. I talked about the harassment that I went through with my child's stepmother. I was able to talk about the affair.

Before I knew it, I let all of that out. My therapist advised me to identify my pain points and the people involved so that eventually I could confront them about it. The people that were on my list were my mom, my dad, my two daughters and my wife. I sat down got in my journal and identify my pain points with each of the people that I needed to confront. I decided to start with my dad first.

Pain Points with Dad:

1. Figure out what he did & how it impacted me.

   - Physically absent
     o Telephone dad
     o Saw him far & few in between
     o We don't know each other.

2. Impact

   - I didn't take you seriously as an authority figure.
   - Made me think I didn't really have a dad.

  i. I got used to you not being around.

  ii. Felt like you didn't want me or didn't have time for me.

3. As an Adult

- You told me to take a year off after I graduated.
    - i. Bad advice
- I applied to college, and you didn't believe me when I told you.
- When I needed our help, you acted like you didn't want to help.
- You always lecture me.
    - i. You should have done this when I was a kid.
- I asked you to help me with the kids and be a father figure to them because their dads weren't in their lives. You said you would, but you didn't.
- You said you wanted a relationship with me but all you did was fuss.
- You always want me to visit you, but you never want to come to me.
- When I tell you about the kid's behaviors, it seemed that you didn't believe me.
- You lectured me about my parenting, and you weren't a good one to me.
- You don't want to hear how the kid's behaviors affected/affects me.
    - i. You don't listen to understand.
- You blame me for not knowing your side of the family.
    - i. I've always felt like an outsider.

- I feel like you don't respect me as an adult.
    i.   You talk to me as if I'm a child.
- You said you wanted to spend more time.
    i.   I had a brunch especially for you and you didn't show up.
- You upset me when you call to lecture me about the girls.

I spoke to my dad about everything listed above. We talked for over two hours. We cried, apologized to each other, and promised to do better. Since writing this book, my dad and I are closer than we ever have been. We talk and visit frequently, and I am planning a family dinner with the entire family soon. We'll also be taking family pictures, something he's been asking to do for a very long time.

Pain Points with Mom:

1. Figure out what she did and how it impacted me:
    a.   Physical abuse
    b.   Had different men (boyfriends) around us.
    c.   We moved all the time.
    d.   Didn't show love (hugs, verbal)
    e.   Didn't pay attention to me.
    f.   Didn't teach me about life.
    g.   Things Dad said about you:
        i.   You asked my dad to give up his rights so your new husband could adopt me.
        ii. You wouldn't let me see my dad as often as he wanted to
2. Impact

   a. Cycle of me disciplining my kids

   b. Didn't think you liked/loved me.

   c. Didn't have a consistent male figure in my life.

   d. Had to constantly adjust to new surroundings.

   e. Didn't know how to show love to myself, my kids, or anyone else.

   f. I was angry all the time.

   g. I experienced things that I shouldn't have at an early age.

   h. I had low self-esteem.

3. As an Adult:

   a. Learned love from someone else.

   b. Low self-esteem

   c. Didn't know how to deal with my emotions.

   d. Wasn't good to myself.

I knew that when I confronted my mom about what was listed above, she wouldn't be open and honest in return, and she wasn't. She had an excuse or denied things that were later found to be true. She did admit that she abused me because one of her older friends told her to. Her response was, "You turned out just fine."

I still must take my mom in doses. We aren't close. She has her own battles and demons that she needs to face, so I can't expect her to help me with mine anymore. It is what it is.

It took me a year to be in therapy and to be able to face acknowledge and essentially begin the healing process. The healing process for me meant to also speak to my children and my wife.

As of the writing of this book I have rekindled my relationship with my oldest daughter. There was an attempt to at least talk with my youngest daughter, but it did not work out well. I invited her to attend therapy sessions with me, but she never responded. I'm not opposed to rekindling our relationship however, she will have to make them next move.

Through therapy and journaling, I was able to look inside myself and fix myself as well. The healing process is a journey that I take every day.

As we journey through the captivating pages of "Quiet As Kept," we are not only invited into Shawnti Refuge's personal narrative but also into a world of profound life lessons. These additional chapters — "Be True to Yourself," "Pursuing Joy + Fulfillment," "Power of Prosperity," and "Showing Yourself More Love" — serve as beacons of wisdom and guidance beyond Shawnti's remarkable story.

Each of these chapters is a treasure trove of insights, meant to inspire and empower you to navigate your own life's journey. They stand as pillars of resilience, growth, and self-discovery, offering a roadmap to authenticity, happiness, and success. With these lessons, we aim to accompany you on your quest to live a life filled with purpose and fulfillment.

As you delve into these chapters, may you find the inspiration to embrace your uniqueness, pursue your passions, and unlock the power of prosperity and self-love within. Shawnti's story is a testament to the strength of the human spirit, and these lessons are our gift to you, our cherished readers, to help you flourish in your own life's narrative.

With gratitude and anticipation,

Shawntie Refuge,

159

Chapter ELEVEN

PURSUING JOY AND FULFILLMENT

Life is a journey full of ups and downs, twists and turns, and unexpected surprises. Along the way, we encounter different experiences and challenges that shape who we are and what we value. And while everyone's journey is unique, there is one thing that we all have in common: the pursuit of joy and fulfillment. To be true to ourselves means being authentic in who we are and what we want. It means pursuing the things that bring us joy and fulfillment rather than what society or others tell us we should want. When we are true to ourselves, we live in alignment with our values and passions and are more likely to find happiness and success. However, pursuing joy and fulfillment is not always easy. It requires us to take risks and step outside of our comfort zones. It may mean letting go of things that no longer serve us or trying something new and unfamiliar. But when we do, the rewards can be immense. When we pursue joy and fulfillment, we open ourselves up to new experiences and opportunities. We may discover new passions, make new connections, or learn something new about ourselves. And even if we face challenges or setbacks along the way, we have the resilience and inner strength to keep going. It's important to note that pursuing joy and fulfillment doesn't mean ignoring our responsibilities or neglecting our obligations. It simply means making time for the things that truly matter to us and prioritizing our own happiness and well-being.

Whether it's pursuing a new career, taking up a new hobby, or traveling to a new destination, there is no one right way to pursue joy and fulfillment. What's important is that we take the time to reflect on what truly brings us happiness and fulfillment, and then take action to pursue those things. If you are feeling stuck or unfulfilled, remember that you have the power to create a life that brings you joy and fulfillment. Be true to yourself and pursue the things that light you up inside. It may not always be easy, but the journey will be worth it. And when you look back on your life, you'll know that you lived it on your own terms, pursuing joy and fulfillment every step of the way.

As we pursue joy and fulfillment, it's important to also be mindful of the journey itself. Life is not just about reaching the destination, but also about the experiences we have and the lessons we learn along the way.

When we pursue our passions and engage in activities that bring us joy, we develop a deeper sense of self-awareness and self-acceptance. We learn more about who we are and what we value, and we become more confident in our ability to create the life we want.

And even when we face challenges or setbacks, we can learn from those experiences and use them as opportunities for growth and learning. We develop resilience and inner strength, and we become better equipped to handle whatever life throws our way.

Ultimately, pursuing joy and fulfillment is about creating a life that feels authentic and meaningful to us. It's about living in alignment with our values and passions and finding purpose and fulfillment in the things we do. To anyone who may be struggling to find joy and fulfillment in their life, know that it's never too late to start. Take the time to reflect on what truly brings you happiness and fulfillment, and then take action to pursue those things. And remember, the journey itself is just as important as the destination. Enjoy the ride, and trust in yourself and your ability to create the life you want.

Chapter TWELVE

BE TRUE TO YOURSELF

As we navigate through life, we often find ourselves constantly seeking approval and validation from those around us. Whether it's from our family, friends, or society as a whole, we can feel like we need to constantly prove ourselves and our worth. But the truth is, we don't owe anyone anything. We don't need to prove ourselves to anyone, whether they're related to us by blood or not. Our happiness and our sense of self-worth should come from within, not from the opinions of others. In the face of societal pressures and expectations, it can be easy to lose sight of who we truly are and what makes us happy. We may feel like we need to conform to certain standards or expectations in order to fit in or be accepted. But the reality is, trying to please others at the expense of our own happiness and wellbeing is a recipe for disaster. Instead, we need to stay true to ourselves and do what makes us happy. Whether it's pursuing a certain career, engaging in a particular hobby, or simply living life on our own terms, we should prioritize our own happiness and fulfillment above all else. That means not feeling guilty for pursuing our passions or doing what brings us joy, even if it doesn't fit with what others expect of us. It means letting go of the need to constantly prove ourselves and instead focusing on our own happiness and self-growth.

At the end of the day, life is too short to spend it trying to please others or living up to their expectations. We owe it to ourselves to be true to who we are and pursue the things that truly make us happy, regardless of what anyone else thinks. Of course, being true to ourselves can be easier said than done. It takes courage and self-awareness to embrace our individuality and let go of the need for external validation. But when we do, the rewards are immense. We begin to live life on our own terms, pursuing our passions and engaging in activities that bring us joy and fulfillment. We start to develop a deeper sense of self-awareness and self-acceptance, and we become more resilient in the face of adversity.

Being true to ourselves also means setting healthy boundaries and saying no to things that don't align with our values or make us happy. It means being honest with ourselves and those around us, even if it may be uncomfortable or difficult.

And while it's important to consider the perspectives and feelings of others, ultimately, our own happiness and wellbeing should be our top priority. By prioritizing our own needs and desires, we set the foundation for a fulfilling and authentic life.

So, to anyone who may feel like they need to prove themselves to others, remember that you are enough exactly as you are. You don't need to conform to anyone else's expectations or standards. You are worthy of love, respect, and happiness simply by being yourself. Embrace your uniqueness and let go of the need for external validation. Be true to yourself and pursue the things that bring you joy and fulfillment. In doing so, you'll create a life that is truly your own, full of meaning, purpose, and happiness.

So, let us embrace our uniqueness and celebrate our individuality. Blood or not, we have nothing to prove to anyone. Let us be and do what makes us happy and find joy and fulfillment in our own lives.

IN THIS SEASON I WILL PROSPER IN WHATEVER I DO!

Life is full of seasons, each with its own unique challenges and opportunities. But no matter what season we find ourselves in, we all have the power to prosper in whatever we do. To prosper means to thrive and grow in a way that is aligned with our values and goals. It means being successful in our endeavors and finding meaning and purpose in the things we do.

However, prospering doesn't just happen overnight. It takes hard work, dedication, and a positive mindset. We need to believe in ourselves and our abilities and be willing to put in the effort to achieve our goals. When we approach life with a mindset of prosperity, we open ourselves up to new opportunities and possibilities. We become more confident in our abilities, and we attract positivity and abundance into our lives. And while we may still face challenges and setbacks along the way, we have the resilience and inner strength to keep going. We see every obstacle as an opportunity to learn and grow, and we stay focused on our goals and dreams.

Prosperity is not just about financial success or material wealth. It's about creating a life that feels meaningful and fulfilling to us. It's about pursuing our passions and living in alignment with our values and goals.

To anyone who may be struggling to find prosperity in their life, know that you have the power to create the life you want. Believe in yourself and your abilities and stay focused on your goals and dreams. And remember, prosperity is not just about what you achieve, but also about who you become in the process. This season, make the commitment to prosper in whatever you do. Trust in yourself and your ability to achieve greatness and embrace the abundance and positivity that life has to offer. When you approach life with a mindset of prosperity, you'll create a life that is truly fulfilling and meaningful.

As we strive to prosper in our lives, it's important to remember that prosperity is not just about achieving our goals, but also about giving back to others. When we experience success and abundance in our own lives, we have the power to uplift and empower others to do the same. One way to do this is by using our success and resources to help others. Whether it's through charitable giving, volunteering, or mentoring, we can use our prosperity to make a positive impact in the lives of others. We can also inspire others by sharing our own stories of overcoming adversity and achieving success. By sharing our journey with others, we can encourage them to believe in themselves and their abilities, and to pursue their own dreams and aspirations.

Ultimately, prosperity is not just about personal success, but also about creating a better world for all. When we prosper in our own lives, we have the power to create positive change and make a difference in the lives of others. So, as we enter this new season, let us commit to prospering in whatever we do. Let us believe in ourselves and our abilities and stay focused on our goals and dreams. And let us use our prosperity to uplift and empower others and create a brighter future for all.

THIS SEASON IS CALLED ELEVATION

L ife is full of seasons, each with its own unique challenges and opportunities. And this season, we are called to embrace a new level of growth and transformation. This season is called elevation.

Elevation is about taking our lives to the next level and reaching new heights of success and fulfillment. It's about shedding the old and embracing the new and stepping into our true potential and purpose.

To elevate our lives, we need to be willing to take risks and step outside of our comfort zones. We may need to let go of things that no longer serve us or challenge our limiting beliefs and self-doubt. But when we do, we open ourselves up to new possibilities and opportunities for growth.

Elevation is not just about achieving material success or recognition. It's about becoming the best version of ourselves and living in alignment with our values and purpose. It's about finding meaning and fulfillment in the things we do and using our talents and abilities to make a positive impact in the world. And while the journey of elevation may not always be easy, it is always worth it. We may face challenges and setbacks along the way, but these experiences help us to grow and become stronger and more resilient. To anyone who may be feeling stuck or unfulfilled in their lives, know that this season is your opportunity to elevate. Embrace the journey of growth and transformation, and trust in yourself and your abilities to achieve greatness.

Remember that elevation is not just about what you achieve, but also about who you become in the process. It's about living a life that is authentic, meaningful, and fulfilling, and making a positive impact in the world around us. This season, make the commitment to elevate your life in every way possible. Embrace the new opportunities and possibilities that come your way and stay focused on your goals and purpose. And when you look back on this season, you'll know that you lived it to the fullest, and embraced the season of elevation with courage, strength, and determination. As we embark on this season of elevation, it's important to stay focused on our goals and purpose. We need to have a clear vision of what we want to achieve and take consistent action to make it happen.

One way to stay focused on our goals is by setting specific, measurable, and achievable targets. This allows us to track our progress and stay motivated along the way. We can also break down our goals into smaller, more manageable steps, which helps to reduce overwhelm and increase our sense of accomplishment. It's also important to surround ourselves with people who support and encourage our growth and transformation. We need to be intentional about the relationships we cultivate and the communities we engage with and seek out those who inspire and uplift us. And as we move forward on our journey of elevation, we need to be willing to adapt and pivot when necessary. Life is full of unexpected twists and turns, and we may need to change course or adjust our plans along the way. But when we remain flexible and open to new possibilities, we allow ourselves to grow and evolve in new and exciting ways. Whoever may be feeling stuck or uncertain about their future, know that this season is your opportunity to elevate. Embrace the journey of growth and transformation, and trust in yourself and your abilities to achieve greatness. Remember that elevation is not just about what you achieve, but also about who you become in the process. It's about living a life that is authentic, meaningful, and fulfilling, and making a positive impact in the world around us.

This Season Is Called Elevation

Chapter

FIFTEEN

SHOW YOURSELF MORE LOVE

Self-love is the foundation for a happy and fulfilling life. When we love ourselves, we are more confident in our abilities, more resilient in the face of adversity, and more able to create the life we want.

Unfortunately, many of us struggle to love ourselves fully. We may have been conditioned to believe that putting ourselves first is selfish, or we may have experienced negative messages or criticism from others that have caused us to doubt our worth and value. But the truth is, showing ourselves love is not selfish or egotistical. It's an act of self-care and self-respect, and it's essential to our overall well-being. To show ourselves more love, we need to be intentional about the messages we give ourselves. We need to speak to ourselves with kindness and compassion and focus on our strengths and accomplishments rather than our flaws and shortcomings.

We also need to prioritize our own needs and desires and make time for activities that bring us joy and fulfillment. Whether it's taking a long bath, reading a good book, or pursuing a creative hobby, we need to make self-care a priority in our lives. And when we do experience setbacks or challenges, we need to practice self-compassion and give ourselves grace. We need to recognize that we are all imperfect beings, and that making mistakes or experiencing failure is a natural part of the human experience. Take the time to reflect on the messages you give yourself and make a conscious effort to replace negative self-talk with positive affirmations.

Make self-care a priority in your life and prioritize your own needs and desires. And when you experience setbacks or challenges, practice self-compassion and give yourself grace. Remember that showing yourself love is not selfish or egotistical. It's an act of self-care and self-respect, and it's essential to your overall well-being. So, show yourself more love today, and every day. You deserve it.

As we learn to love ourselves more, we also become better equipped to love and care for others. When we are filled with love and compassion for ourselves, we are more able to extend that love and compassion to those around us. We become better listeners, more empathetic, and more able to provide support and encouragement to those in need. We also become better role models for others and inspire them to love and care for themselves in the same way. But perhaps most importantly, when we show ourselves more love, we are able to live more authentically and confidently. We are able to pursue our passions and dreams without fear or hesitation and live a life that is true to our values and purpose. So, to anyone who may be struggling to love themselves fully, know that you are worthy and deserving of love and respect. Take the time to show yourself more love every day and make self-care a priority in your life. And as you do, remember that you are not only showing love to yourself, but also to those around you. You are inspiring others to love and care for themselves in the same way and creating a ripple effect of positivity and compassion in the world.

So, show yourself more love today, and every day. You deserve it. And remember, when you love yourself fully, you are able to live a life that is authentic, fulfilling, and true to your purpose.

20 QUIET AS KEPT RULES

1. Believe in yourself, even when nobody else does: Trust in your own abilities and never underestimate yourself, even when others may doubt you.

2. Don't be afraid to speak your truth, even when it's uncomfortable: Be honest and open about your experiences, even if it may be difficult to share.

3. Embrace your inner strength and let it guide you through life's challenges: Draw on your inner strength and resilience to help you navigate life's obstacles.

4. Never give up on your dreams - you have the power to make them a reality: Stay committed to your goals and believe in your ability to achieve them.

5. Surround yourself with positive, supportive people who believe in you: Surround yourself with people who lift you up and support you in your journey.

6. Take care of yourself, both physically and mentally: Prioritize your physical and mental health and practice self-care regularly.

7. Don't let others' opinions define you - only you have that power: Stay true to yourself and don't let others' opinions dictate your sense of self-worth.

8. Embrace your mistakes and learn from them - they are opportunities for growth: Don't be afraid to make mistakes - use them as opportunities for learning and growth.

9. Practice forgiveness - not for others, but for your own peace of mind: Let go of grudges and resentment and practice forgiveness to find peace within yourself.

10. Above all, remember that you are worthy of love, respect, and happiness: Believe in your own worthiness and don't settle for anything less.

11. Trust your instincts and follow your intuition - you know what's best for you: Listen to your inner voice and trust yourself to make the right decisions.

12. Set boundaries and stick to them - you deserve to be treated with respect: Set clear boundaries for yourself and others and respect them to maintain your sense of self-worth.

13. Take responsibility for your actions and choices - you have the power to create your own path: Take ownership of your actions and choices and use them to create your own future.

14. Practice self-care regularly - it's essential for your physical and mental wellbeing: Prioritize self-care activities to maintain your physical and mental health and wellbeing.

15. Celebrate your successes, no matter how small they may seem: Recognize and celebrate even the smallest accomplishments to build self-confidence and motivation.

16. Remember that healing is a journey, not a destination - take it one day at a time: Approach healing with patience and understanding, and don't put pressure on yourself to have it all figured out at once.

17. Don't be afraid to ask for help when you need it - it's a sign of strength, not weakness: Seek out help and support when needed and recognize that doing so is a sign of strength, not weakness.

18. Focus on what you can control and let go of what you can't: Focus on the things within your control and let go of the things outside of your control to maintain a sense of inner peace.

19. Use your experiences to help others who may be going through similar struggles: Use your experiences to help others who may be going through similar challenges and be a positive influence in their lives.

20. Believe in your ability to overcome any obstacle and achieve your goals - you are capable of greatness: Have confidence in your own abilities and believe that you have the power to overcome any obstacle and achieve greatness.

CONNECT

WITH

SHAWNTI REFUGE

AT

www.shawntirefugejournals.com

AND ACROSS SOCIAL MEDIA

www.ingramcontent.com/pod-product-compliance
Lightning Source LLC
Chambersburg PA
CBHW041558160726
48006CB00042B/2064